Praise for "What's In Your Sandwich?"

"Jocelyn Giangrande has captured the essence of what women need to build the success they desire in their career. Her use of the "sandwich" methodology adds humor, understandable context, and basic principles that all women will relate to and benefit from. This book will yield growth and enlightenment, irrespective of where a woman is in her career path. The information practicality, pearls of lessons learned, statically facts, and strong dose of truths from "a reality check", comes from a woman who not only has the expertise and experience, but the heart, compassion, and intellect to deliver the message as it should be told."

Earlexia M. Norwood, M.D., Physician-In-Charge
Henry Ford Medical Center-Troy, Henry Ford Health System

"What's in Your Sandwich? is practical, empowering and inspiring! A must read for any woman who wants to start a career, enhance her career or transition her career to an unknown new beginning. *What's in Your Sandwich?* gets the juices flowing again, makes you believe in the possibilities and most importantly, it makes you believe in yourself. Jocelyn Giangrande's approach is fresh and invigorating. Like a cool breeze on a hot, humid day; her words will awaken your senses, stir your spirit and give you the confidence to be all that you can be!"

Monica E. Emerson, Navy Diversity Officer,
U. S. Department of the Navy

D0710826

"The quest to "shatter the glass ceiling" in American business continues to be a perplexing and seemingly unattainable goal for most women. According to a 2010 USA News report, women comprise only 15% of board seats and are 3% of CEOS among Fortune 500 companies. In her book, "What's in Your Sandwich?" Jocelyn Giangrande's creativity and years of successful coaching of young working women provides an insightful and refreshing twist on this age-old dilemma."

Kathy Oswald, Senior Vice President & Chief Human Resources Officer, Henry Ford Health System

Oswald has been featured in Human Resource World's Top 50 HR Executives in the World, Automotive News' 100 Leading Women in the North American Auto Industry and Crain's Detroit Business' Most Influential Women

"Jocelyn Giangrande's book is a must read manual for women wanting to take charge of their careers. Through metaphors, stories and honest advice, she artfully presents the key elements for an empowered approach to excelling in one's career in today's business environment. I wish I had had her guidance earlier in my own career!"

Jacqueline Binkert, Ph.D., Executive Coach and co-author of *Appreciative Coaching: A Positive Process for Change*

The Confident Woman Series™

What's In Your Sandwich?™

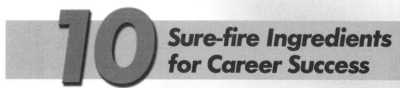

10 **Sure-fire Ingredients for Career Success**

JOCELYN GIANGRANDE

SASHE, LLC | Bloomfield, Michigan

What's In Your Sandwich? 10 Sure-fire Ingredients
for Career Success   .
By Jocelyn Giangrande
Published by SASHE, LLC, Bloomfield, MI 48304

ISBN (13) 978-0-9839816-0-2

Library of Congress Control Number: 2011915629

For information, contact:
Jocelyn Giangrande
jgiangrande@sashewomen.com
www.jocelyngiangrande.com

Editor: Skyla P. Thomas, Pleasant Words, LLC,
www.pleasantwords.net
Cover and Interior Design: LaTanya Orr
Selah Branding and Design LLC, www.iselah.com

Printed in the United States of America

This Book is
Dedicated to—

My loving husband Nick and son Quen.
Both gave 100% support while I wrote this book.

My mother Mildred, sister Angela, and mother-in-law Carol,
for giving all of the love and support I needed.

My family, friends, mentors, and clients, who through their
encouragement and support, gave me the fuel.

To my two favorite teachers, Mr. Gil Congdon,
of Reading Memorial High School, Reading, MA
and Mrs. Hines of St. Ambrose Elementary School, Grosse
Pointe Park, Michigan. Both were exceptional teachers.
Through their influence, I gained a sense
of who I could become.

Special Acknowledgements

A special thanks goes to the leadership of Henry Ford Health System and Hilton Hotels Corporation. It is through their stimulating work environment that my professional, developmental and relational growth soared.

A special thanks to family, friends & mentors…

Cheryl Abaloz
Candy Collins-Adams
Sharifa Alcendor
Terry Barclay
Rodney Bellamy
Holly Bhasin
Kay Burgess
Beth Bruss
Anton Chastang
Gil Congdon (the greatest teacher in the world)
Sylvia Daniels
Bilal Dabaja
Bronwyn Davis
Don Davis
Grace Delia
Brandi Elliott
Monica Emerson
Mr & Mrs. Mike Devins
Shanna Garrison
Michelle Fanroy
Rita Fields
Cathy Flaugher
Rose Glenn
Thomas Groth
Antonia Green
Gerard Van Grinsven
Cynthia Grubbs
John Hayden
Barbara Hamilton
Betsy Hemmings
Lorraine Henry
Sandhya Henry

Maureen Henson
Dee Hunt
Laurie Jensen
Gail Jordan
Najoi Jreige
Angela Kennedy
Bill Kerrey
Nabil Khoury
Cydney Koukol
Suzanne Klien
Kathy Macki
Tearza Martin
Lawanda Marshall
Angelene McLaren
Barbara McKee
Katrina McCree
Lisbeth McNabb
Zachary Menges
Tara Michener
Bruce Muma, MD
Veretta Nix
Elexia Norwood M.D.
Kathy Oswald
Tiffany Owens
Bea Paige
Ajay Parikh
Patrick Payne
Bill Peterson
Shanna Reed
Robert Riney
Clarissa Russell
Nancy Schlichting

Saleem Siddiqui
Lawrence Simmons
Sherri Simmons
Terra Siller
Chrishondra Smith
Patty Smith
Richard Smith, M.D.
Dianhann Stanfield
Marlowe Stoudamire
Valencia Stoudamire
Phyllis Taylor
Janice Tessier
Toni Thomas
Kimberly Rath
Monica Rogers
Amy Schultz
Sheri Takacs
Laurita Thomas
Cheryl Trapp
Cami Wacker
Randy Walker
Ken Walker
Rose-Marie Walker
Equilla Wainwright
Pat Ward
Deborah Wilkelis
Deborah Williams & family
Debra Williams
Karen Williams
Leona Williams & family (Auntie)
Kimberly Dawn-Wisdom, M.D.
Tannisha Woods

— And many others not listed…
Thank you… It is nice to be among friends...

Table of Contents

Introduction

Dear Reader,

Do you remember your feelings of accomplishment after you landed your first "real" job? It felt like the start of something big and you believed you were on the road to a promising career.

However, somewhere along the way, your promising career took a turn. Things have moved from promising to challenging. You are no longer optimistic about where you are going. Your confidence has dwindled and you question your next move. On top of all that, you feel unappreciated, overwhelmed and stuck.

If this book caught your eye, you probably are experiencing some of these feelings and you are ready to do something about it. However, if you are like most professional working-women, you don't know where to start.

When it comes to our careers, how is it that we find ourselves stuck and frustrated? Many of my clients talk about feeling this way as I did early in my career. The truth is, today's workplace is challenging and navigating a career is difficult. There aren't roadmaps or practical resources designed to help us plan. Many of us struggle trying to find our way.

Many things contribute to our experiences in the workplace. Over the years, as I helped hundreds of women plan their strategies, I started to see patterns in how we manage our careers. Based on research and through my work, I believe that there are three main reasons why our careers get stuck and get off-track.

The first reason is that many of us lack an understanding of office politics. We often take things personally and don't understand the importance of working our networks and building strategic relationships. This is all part of a successful career strategy.

The second reason is that we don't know how to engage in self-promotion so that others know our worth, our ideas and our accomplishments. Most women shy away from promoting themselves because they see it as distasteful and unnecessary. Instead, we believe our work should speak for itself. Often when it doesn't, we are baffled and feel unappreciated.

Lastly, many of us believe that hard work is key to our success. Therefore, we keep our nose to the grindstone instead of getting out of our offices to build strategic connections and supportive networks. Contrary to common belief, hard work alone is not enough. This was a difficult lesson for me and was an important step in changing my perspective on my career. I learned that in order to advance in the corporate world, it takes much more than hard work to break through. Successful careers are not often built on your experience, performance or hard work. It takes much more to get ahead.

When it comes to our careers, we often struggle alone. Many of us never reach executive levels. The 2010 article, *"The Gender Gap: 10 Surprising Stats on Women in the Workplace,"* reveals the fact that women have not come that far over the last century. Take a look at these stats:

"The Gender Gap: 10 Surprising Stats on Women in the Workplace," Job Profile, February, 2010

1. Women comprise 46% of the total U.S. labor force.
2. Women make only 77.5 cents for every dollar that men earn.
3. The more education a woman has, the greater the disparity in her wages.
4. Women may work longer to receive the promotions that provide access to higher pay.
5. Women business owners employ 35% more people than all the Fortune 500 companies combined.
6. Women account for 46% of the labor force, but 59% of workers making less than $8 an hour.
7. Only 53% of employers provide at least some re-placement pay during periods of maternity leave.
8. Four in ten businesses worldwide have no women in senior management.

9. Women earn less than men in 99% of all occupations.
10. Minority women fare the worst when it comes to equal pay.

This study demonstrates that we need more support, guidance and equal treatment in the workplace. It is up to us to make it happen.

WHAT IT TAKES TO HAVE A SUCCESSFUL CAREER

There are many components that make for a successful career. Through interviews, research and generous support of mentors, I've discovered that there are common characteristics, strategies and principles that contribute to career and business success. Many books are written on the common attributes of leaders and I've read most of them. Although these books are relevant, few tell you how to plan your career strategy in practical steps. That's why I wrote this book. *What's in Your Sandwich?* is designed to help women like you, plan a strategy to get your career moving in the right direction.

Today's workplace requires professionals to take greater responsibility for their individual growth. Therefore, this book is not just about planning a strategy; it is also designed to empower you. It is time for you to take charge of your career and drive it where you want it to go.

WHY A BOOK FOR WOMEN ONLY?

I am confident that this book could help anyone looking to get his or her career on track. Therefore, both men and women will find these strategies relevant. With that said, being a professional woman, with a family, and a demanding job, I have first-hand knowledge of what women face in the workplace. This positions me to better understand our issues, pitfalls and barriers. I also feel a sense of sisterhood to other working women.

At the end of the day, if this book helps men, I am pleased.

If you like this book, share it with friends and family! As cliché as it may sound, it does take a village for all to succeed. So, do your part and share the knowledge. When we share the knowledge, we all win.

Your coach, mentor and friend,

Jocelyn

P.S. The strategies outlined may also be applied to business success as well. So, if you have desires to be an entrepreneur, these strategies will help you too.

Take care!

"Your future depends on many things, but mostly on you."
- Unknown

It is in the spirit of this quote, that I write this book.

-Jocelyn Giangrande

chapter one

The Making of My Sandwich

"Your future depends on many things,
but mostly on you." - Unknown

MY CAREER JOURNEY

From an early age, I have always been ambitious. I approached my career the same way. Career progression and development have always been high on my value's list. So, when my career started showing signs of stagnation, frustration began to creep in. Soon, I found myself wondering where my career was going and what was next for me. However, I am getting ahead of myself, so let me start by sharing where I've been.

My early career started out with great promise. Being an ambitious young woman, my bosses were often impressed with my dedication, energy and consistency. Therefore, I moved through entry-level management with great ease. My work ethic was built around working hard and proving that I had what it took to get the job done. My eyes were always on the next position and I was willing "to work for it." I was what you would call "a hard worker."

My hard work moved me through organizations, winning awards and accolades for work well done. I was ready to take on the world. Eventually, I was fast–tracked and on my way.

My early climb started with getting new responsibility after new responsibility. Each time my boss gave me more responsibility, my confidence soared. I set out to prove that I could handle the workload by working around the clock and showing them that I had what it took and that they could count on me to get it done.

I went from team leader, to manager, to director, to vice president. I studied many industries to ensure that I remained current, did my homework before meetings and took advantage of every training opportunity offered. My career development profile was jammed-packed with education and certificates. When you entered my office, you would have been overwhelmed with numerous certificates, diplomas and awards displayed. Many of my colleagues called it my "wall of fame."

My consistent performance and drive moved me right up the ladder and I knew I had made it when I secured an executive position. Then, just when I thought I had finally made it, out of nowhere, it felt like someone put up a brick wall and I ran right into it. Suddenly my career, which had been ascending, came to a screeching halt. Although the halt seemed sudden, in reflection, there were warning signs that a wall was up ahead. However, I did not see it coming.

Once I hit the wall, I began assessing what had happened, where I went wrong and what to do next. Soon, I started ramping up my reading on leadership and I read every book I could find on the topic. I also studied other famous leaders from around the world. My quest also included studying the successful leaders around me, both within my organization and throughout my network.

After comparing my leadership traits to those who were successful in sustaining high ranks, I discovered something interesting. I found that my career strategy was actually missing key sure-fire ingredients to sustain at the executive level. It was evident that I needed to change my strategy.

WHAT WAS MISSING

When I tell women about my career progression, they are usually quite impressed. They see the achievements I've made and my climb up the corporate ladder. However, they don't know the whole story.

Interestingly enough, although I was fast-tracked early in my career, I didn't have many mentors and I never had a sponsor. Little did I know, without mentors and a sponsor who advocates and opens doors for you, your career will come to a halt at one time or another, and sometimes, just as I experienced, you even hit a brick wall.

Mentors are imperative to any career strategy. It's your mentors who give the feedback, advice and wisdom, which would take a lifetime to learn on your own. Women, who attempt to learn this on their own, tend to burn out in the process. That is exactly what happened to me.

Without influential mentors, managing my career was like climbing Mt. Everest without the right hiking gear. The higher I got on the ladder, the more challenging my career became. Without someone to help guide me, I was forced to learn many things the hard way. Learning the hard way is actually very common among women. In fact, just like me, many women admit to learning how to navigate on their own, all without the guidance of someone experienced to show them the way.

To my amazement, I also found that I was lacking other key ingredients. Self-promotion and effective relationships were missing. I learned that these are sure-fire ingredients for a sustainable and successful career. I believe that the lack of these key ingredients is why I hit the brick wall. It wasn't until I added these sure-fire ingredients into my career strategy, that my career regained its momentum.

GIVING BACK

During my climb up the corporate ladder, other women always sought me out for support with their careers. Although I wasn't mentored, I enjoyed mentoring many women and sharing my lessons-learned. In fact, I usually had upwards of eight to ten active mentees at any given time.

Eventually, I discovered I had a passion for helping women to look at things from a different perspective and to help them navigate their careers with confidence. The knowledge I gained from my own experience, I shared with others.

Over time, my name got around, and I found myself with so many mentees, I didn't have enough hours in a day to see them all. Every time I helped one woman, she would tell a friend to seek me out also. I began receiving emails from people stating that they were referred by: "so-and-so" and they wanted to know if we could meet for coffee or lunch. Eventually, my evenings and Saturdays were filled with women looking for career advice, coaching and mentorship. I had to start meeting them in groups just to keep up with the demand. I lived in coffee shops and I am still surprised that I was not charged for leasing space.

After a decade of mentoring women, I realized that the majority of women are missing some of the same key ingredients in their careers as I did early on. Many women are navigating their workplaces without adequate roadmaps, without sponsorship and without the right tools. The lack of these ingredients contributes to stagnant careers, roadblocks and eventually frustration. Ironically, many of my mentees were unaware of what they were lacking and were baffled when their careers were derailed as well.

WHERE I AM GOING

To be honest, I am not 100% sure where I am going. And, that is fine with me. I am enjoying the journey of self-discovery and plan to let my passion drive me forward. This book is the start of my drive and passion.

The truth is, I love helping others. I love a challenge; I love problem solving and most of all I love finding solutions. There is nothing in this world as great as having had a part in helping to overcome an obstacle, leverage talents and propel careers. No other work is more fulfilling to me.

What I do know is that I am on a mission to help women advance their careers and empower them to take charge. I look forward to seeing what is next and how I may continue to support you on your career journey.

A PEANUT BUTTER AND JELLY SANDWICH STORY

One day, a team member of mine asked to speak to me about a matter that she thought deserved attention. I have always maintained an open door policy, so I invited her in my office to talk. It was apparent that she was very concerned, and when she began to speak, it was also apparent that she was angry.

Once seated, she proceeded to tell me that many of the employees on the floor whom also happen to be women, had been coming to her to vent about working in the department. According to her, they were not happy about their future at the company. Although none of these women reported to me directly, she thought I would be a good person in which to share their concerns.

According to her, many of the women felt that they were not going anywhere on their jobs. Since many had been loyal to the organization by devoting several years of hard work, they expected something in return. They wanted to be appreciated; they wanted more advancement opportunities and they wanted more development. She also told me that she was tired of hearing these complaints every day, and she was hoping that I could help them.

Although she was talking about other women, her body language told me she felt the same way. Not only were all of the women on the floor frustrated, so was she.

"Why is it that these leaders around here don't care about their people?" she asked. "I feel sorry for the people who have worked their butts off for this company and no one seems to notice or care." "On top of that," she continued, "we get paid peanuts."

She went on with stating how she felt sorry for the secretary on the suite who she believed was underpaid for what she did. And she also talked about how another woman who was a customer service representative was the only one on the team with a college degree and she could not get the promotion she applied for. She went on and on for about 15 minutes without taking a breath.

Finally, after realizing that I had not said a word, she stopped herself and asked me if I thought she was crazy. I stated, "of course I don't." She then asked me the question I had been waiting for:

"Why is it that some people get ahead around here and others don't?" I paused for a moment and answered, "I understand that you and the women on the floor are frustrated about your careers. However, I suggest that you first look at how you are promoting yourselves and ask yourselves what are you doing that may be causing you to be overlooked. Are you being professional; are you demonstrating that you are organized; what impression is your workspace sending, what is your reputation and are you going after the right positions?"

I finished by saying, "I am not sure what the definitive answer is, as each person is different." "However, I continued, "the first step to finding the answer, starts with having the courage to look inward first."

I must admit, my response totally caught her by surprise, leaving her looking like a deer in the headlights. She paused for a moment, and then looked down at the floor. When she raised her head, she asked, "Do you think what is happening around here is our fault?"

I replied, "There's probably enough fault to go around, but because we are only capable of controlling ourselves and we are only capable of knowing what we bring to a problem, I'd certainly start there first."

She left my office stating that she would have to think about what I said and asked to continue our conversation once she had done so. I agreed.

I share this story because it highlights the feelings of many women in the workplace. Many of us are frustrated in our careers, our organizations and in our future. So, I ask you, what are we going to do about it?

MANAGING YOUR CAREER

What I learned most during my career is that managing your career is your responsibility and yours alone. And whether you know it or not, your future is mostly in your hands. Therefore, if your career is advancing or declining, you play a major role in what is playing out. I know that may sound harsh to some, and to others, it may not seem fair. However, if you are willing to look inward and be honest with yourself, you will agree that you are the center of your career story.

When I tell others that they have control over their careers, many have a difficult time accepting that responsibility. They see it as a monumental task, and often they do not know where to start taking control. However, believe it or not, having control over your career is the best thing that can happen to you. When you take your career into your own hands, you become the driver. Better yet, when you take responsibility, you no longer have to be a victim, you no longer have to feel trapped, and you can set yourself free. And, equipped with the right motivation, you can take your career where you want it to go; thus, freeing you to take advantage of your many options. And yes, you do have options.

What are your options? Well, your options are very much dependant on what's in your sandwich.

What does a sandwich have to do with building a career strategy? ...A lot.

Once when I was mentoring a friend's daughter, in an attempt to explain to her what she was missing in her career strategy, I used a sandwich metaphor. I told her, "Building your career is just like building your favorite sandwich. In your favorite sandwich, you can put anything you want in it. However, the sandwich is only as good as the ingredients."

Noticing that she was following me, I continued with the metaphor:

**"There are key ingredients every woman needs
in her career just like there are key ingredients
in a good sandwich."**

I started to outline suggested ingredients for her career sandwich. Ingredients such as a good reputation, current skills, etc. were important to her strategy. Eventually catching on, she jumped in and started helping me by throwing in a few ingredients herself.

Soon we found ourselves conducting an inventory of her current career sandwich. Our work uncovered that she had a few key ingredients in her sandwich already. She was lucky to already have a mentor and she possessed great communication skills. However, she was missing several other ingredients that were crucial to her success. We made a plan on how she would obtain those missing ingredients and "build her own career sandwich."

As we continued to meet, whenever we got together, she started by saying, "I have been building my sandwich." That was the start of what I now call the "career strategy sandwich" theory.

BUILDING YOUR CAREER SANDWICH

When it comes to a sandwich, I assume that most women know how to make one. Believe me, I do understand the danger of assuming. However, I am confident that if you don't know how to make one, you could learn pretty quickly. Therefore, I chose the sandwich analogy to show that if armed with the right ingredients, planning a career strategy can be just as easy.

When making a sandwich, everyone knows that the sandwich is only as good as the ingredients you put into it, rights? Well, it is the same with your career. Just like a sandwich, the best careers are made with care, with the best ingredients and are kept fresh over time. And just like a sandwich, your career is portable and you can cater it to your needs, desires and dreams. Therefore, just as the best sandwiches are stacked with great stuff; so should your career.

SO, WHAT'S IN YOUR SANDWICH?

When I set out to build my sandwich, I started by evaluating what other successful leaders had in theirs. I studied exceptional leaders, read hundreds of books, as well as received mentorship from generous executives and business people. Based on that knowledge, I was able to develop my list of the ten sure-fire ingredients I found critical to their career success. They are as follows:

Jocelyn's 10 Sure-fire Ingredients for Career Success

1. Self-Confidence
2. Leveraged Talents
3. Golden Reputation
4. Effective Self-promotion
5. Supportive Networks
6. Diverse Mentors & Sponsors
7. Positive Relationships
8. Exceptional Communication Skills
9. Strategy and Execution
10. Influence Over Others

These ingredients form the core of my work with clients to ensure that their careers stay on track and continue moving forward. At times, my clients will tell me that they already know that these ingredients are important, however, they just want to figure out how to get ahead. I realize that you may be saying the same. However, what most women underestimate is the importance of having these ingredients demonstrated in their sandwich. Therefore, they are not currently in their career strategy and their careers suffer.

Just like a sandwich, you don't have to have all of the ingredients to have a good one. However, chances are that your career and sandwich gets better when you add more to it. Therefore, when you are cooking up your career, the more ingredients you acquire, the more powerful your career will be.

HOW TO USE THIS BOOK

Sure-fire Ingredients: There are 10 sure-fire ingredients that every woman should have in her career strategy. Each of these ingredients are discussed in its own chapter. There you will find practical steps, tips and information on how to build that ingredient into your sandwich.

The beauty of **What's In Your Sandwich?** is that you may build your sandwich any way you wish. Some of you may already have some of the ingredients working for you. Others may want to enhance them or add new ones. Therefore, you can choose to read the book from cover-to-cover, by ingredient, or use it as a reference guide. My suggestion is to read it cover-to-cover first, then use it as a reference guide to stay fresh.

Executive Chefs: In this book, you will find many things besides career advice and guidance. Each chapter starts with the career journey and perspectives of an Executive Chef. Each Chef (they are not real chefs), are actually successful leaders whom I hand-selected due to their professional success and demonstrated proficiency in selected ingredients. These chefs share their personal stories and experiences as they climbed the corporate ladder. They are leaders in communities and organizations, successful entrepreneurs, mentors and individuals whom I have connected with during my career journey.

Sandwich Stories: You will also find different sandwich stories (named after popular sandwiches) sprinkled throughout the book. These stories are derived from many of the lessons I learned along the way. They also come from the experiences of my clients and women I encountered through my coaching, mentoring and speaking engagements. These stories are designed to give you a viewpoint into the experiences of women and how lacking or possessing key ingredients impacted their careers.

Extra Toppings: Each chapter ends with extra toppings to enhance your sandwich. These are additional tips and reminders to help you embellish your career strategy. They are just a little something to take away with you on your journey to career success.

Quotes: Throughout the book and at the beginning of each chapter, you will find my quotes of motivation, encouragement and things to ponder. These quotes are also captured in the resources section of this book.

Lets' get cooking...

Setting Up Your Kitchen for Success

"Advancing your career is a competitive sport. To increase your wins, you must get your mindset ready to compete." -Jocelyn

SETTING UP YOUR KITCHEN

Before you start to cook, setting up your kitchen for success is usually the first step to making great dishes. The same is true for your career. Before planning a great career strategy, it is important to set up your mind for success. I call it 'setting up your kitchen.'

Let's start with getting into the right frame of mind. Below are the career mindset steps to help you get started:

STEP 1: Understand that Career Advancement is a Competitive Sport

The first step is having a clear understanding that career advancement 'is not' a passive sport. Career advancement is competitive and you cannot advance your career without taking action.

THE COMPETITIVE MINDSET

We seldom, if ever, think of our careers as a competition. Chances are also true that we never look at our career as a type of sport. We honestly believe that if we are smart enough and we do our part, we will be rewarded accordingly. We wrongly believe that our contributions to the company will be demonstrated by us winning promotions and receiving acknowledgements for a job well done. If you begin to think of your career as a competitive sport, you will treat your career quite differently.

The fact that men tend to both play and follow competitive sports more so than women, gives them an advantage in the workplace.   An important lesson competitive sports teach is that in a competition, not everyone can be a winner. This concept is important because it takes away the personal feelings that go with losing and instead, creates a continuous learning perspective. It also promotes exercising other aspects besides just knowledge or performance to win. If one way doesn't work, being competitive means that you try another tactic.

Continuous improvement is important to growing careers. It is because of this, that I often tell women to learn from mistakes, shortcomings and losses. Therefore, when you lose out on a promotion, reflect on what may have contributed to that loss. That's what athletes do when they lose a game. After losing, they head to the locker room to debrief and prepare for the next one. This is an example of a competitive mindset.

When it comes to a competitive mindset, women often ask me, "What does having a competitive mindset really mean?" Many women that I encounter work hard at educating themselves, gaining great experience and doing excellent work. Therefore, when I tell them that they are not competitive, they are baffled. Although education, experience and hard work are important, that alone will not ensure advancement. Advancement will also require you to be aggressive, break rules and take risks. Just like in sports, athletes try all types of approaches to win. That is competition.

When we were growing up, we, as women, were expected to learn how to get along and not make enemies. I know I also learned early on that rules were not meant to be broken. Most of our play as children involved various forms of passive play.

Pat Heim in her book *Hardball for Women, Winning at the Game of Business*, talks about the lessons that boys learn early on that helps them succeed in business. These lessons are as follows:

◎ Always do what the coach says
◎ Competition is the name of the game
◎ How to be a good team player

- ◎ How to be a leader
- ◎ How to be aggressive or posture aggressiveness
- ◎ How to take criticism and praise
- ◎ How to stay focused on the goal
- ◎ Winning is all that matters
- ◎ How to have a game plan

On the contrary, take a look at what Heim's describes as the lessons girls learn early in life. They are as follows:
- ◎ How to play one-on-one
- ◎ How to get along
- ◎ How to be fair to everyone
- ◎ How to engage in play as a process
- ◎ How to negotiate differences
- ◎ How to keep the power dead even

Remember the "Peanut Butter and Jelly" story about my team member and her anger that the women in the department worked very hard and didn't 'feel' that they were appreciated? Can you tell me if those women were operating with competitive mindsets? If they were, they would try all types of tactics to get in the game and not rely on their managers to set the course.

Heim also highlights what women must do to be competitive:
- ◎ Be assertive without being obnoxious
- ◎ Display confidence
- ◎ Engage in self-promotion
- ◎ Lead both men and women and recognize the differences between them
- ◎ Use "power talk" language to your advantage

Competition is action in motion. When you approach your career as a competition, it causes you to get in the driver's seat and to do what needs to be done to win the game. You must learn from your setbacks and try different approaches. There is nothing passive about taking charge of your career. You must take action if you wish to move forward.

STEP 2: Understand the Playing Field

Many of us work every day and never truly examine the landscape. Therefore, we don't understand the playing field. One example I see playing out is that many women continue to believe that the playing field is equal. We continue this belief even when we are continuously confronted with hard cold evidence that it is not. Despite the evidence, in our hearts we want to believe the contrary, believing that life should be fair.

It is important to realize that in business, there is no such thing as a level playing field. Many people have advantages that others do not. That is life. However, you can position yourself to be competitive and get in the game as well.

To advance in the 21st century, far more emphasis will be placed on having a pool of professionals who will take greater control and responsibility for their own individual growth. It is imperative now more than ever that you take full advantage of your innate talents to stay competitive.

You must maintain:

- ◎ A commitment to your career destiny
- ◎ The ability to set goals
- ◎ An openness to feedback
- ◎ An orientation to continuous learning

STEP 3: Understand Why People Fail

You can learn a great deal from failures. In fact, many of our most valuable lessons come to us as a result of failures. I know that is true for me. However, when you are planning your strategy, it is important to understand some of the pitfalls that have derailed careers so that you can attempt to avoid them in yours.

Jack M. Zufelt, in his landmark book, *The DNA of Success*, created the following list of why we fail:

- ◎ We don't know what we truly want.
- ◎ We buy into conventional success methodologies and self help thinking.
- ◎ We fail to seek or utilize qualified mentors.
- ◎ We expect too much too soon.
- ◎ We fail to seek feedback and make course corrections.
- ◎ We focus more on what we lack than on the strengths, assets and resources we possess.
- ◎ We procrastinate and succumb to the paralysis of analysis.
- ◎ We move forward without a plan or strategy and then quit too soon.

When I first read Zufelt's list of why people fail, I found myself nodding in agreement as I recounted moments in my career when I was guilty of some of the things he outlined. Did you recognize some things about your own approach in his list?

A pitfall we also experience while charting our career is expecting too much too soon. Having an expectation of moving quickly can derail advancement. The old adage of 'good things come to those who wait' applies here. I am not discounting the few who become 'over night successes,' but they are few and far between.

John Beeson, of Beeson Consulting, writing in the *Harvard Business Review; June 2009*, **'Managing Yourself, Why You didn't Get That Promotion,'** provides us with 'food for thought' when he states that advancement decisions fall into the following three categories:

1. The Non-negotiables
2. The De-selection Factors
3. The Core Selection Factors

Although, Beeson's, *Key Factors in Executive Career Advancement,* is a model that was developed for senior managers, its' information is valuable no matter where you are in your career. Although factors do differ slightly at various companies, these factors are commonly found in most.

When it comes to non-negotiables, Beeson's model states that there are three behaviors that you must demonstrate to enter the game. According to Beeson, the factors are:

NON-NEGOTIABLES

Factors that are absolutely necessary for you to be a contender:
- ◎ Demonstrating consistently strong performance
- ◎ Displaying ethics, integrity and character
- ◎ Being driven to lead and to assume higher levels of responsibility

Beeson continues by outlining the factors that get you kicked out of the game. He calls these factors the "De-selection Factors." If you display these behaviors, you may find your entry ticket revoked. The de-selection factors are:

DE-SELECTION FACTORS

Characteristics that prevent you from being considered as a serious candidate:
- ◎ Having weak interpersonal skills
- ◎ Treating others with insensitivity or abrasiveness
- ◎ Putting self-interest above company good
- ◎ Holding a narrow, parochial perspective on the business and the organization

Those who have ambition to reach the executive ranks must demonstrate that they can handle the responsibility. Therefore, according to Beeson, they must demonstrate the "Core Selection Factors." They are as follows:

CORE SELECTION FACTORS

Capabilities that breed other's confidence in your ability to succeed at the senior level:

◎ Setting direction and thinking strategically.

◎ Building and continually upgrading a strong executive team.

◎ Managing implementation without getting involved at too low a level of detail.

◎ Building the capacity for innovation and change; knowing when new ways of doing business are required.

◎ Getting things done across internal boundaries.

◎ Growing and developing as an executive.

Setting up your kitchen is important to cooking great meals. The same is true of your career. Understanding that career advancement is competitive, considering the playing field and recognizing why we fail, is part of that set up. This initial step is an important process to building your career sandwich.

Super Ingredients for Sustained Success

"Most successful women's sandwiches also have three super ingredients in common; a lot of preparation, many opportunities and a bit of luck." -Jocelyn

SUPER INGREDIENTS FOR SUSTAINED SUCCESS

As a 'new' professional, fresh out of graduate school, I recall having this sense of awe for the highly successful. I believed that successful people had this special genius thing bestowed upon them. Looking at those in impressive positions used to leave me wondering, "*How can I get there?*" At times, I remember feeling clueless, thinking that I did not have what it took to get ahead. I often wondered, "What was in their career sandwich that led to their success?"

My research helped bring out three *super ingredients* common among these successful people. I found that the *super ingredients* highly successful people rely on are:

AMOUNT	INGREDIENT
A lot of	**preparation**
Many	**opportunities**
A bit of	**luck**

A LOT OF **PREPARATION**

Defined as a state of being prepared; the action of making something ready for use or service or of getting ready for some occasion; the state of having been made ready before hand; readiness.

MANY **OPPORTUNITIES**

Defined as a good position, chance or prospect; a favorable or advantageous circumstance or combination of circumstances; a possibility due to a favorable combination of circumstances; a favorable or suitable occasion or time.

A BIT OF **LUCK**

Defined as a force that brings good fortune or adversity; the events or circumstances that operate for or against an individual.

I was not the first person to attribute that preparation, opportunity and luck to success. I just confirmed for myself that there is truth to it. Oprah, among other successful people, asserted, *"Luck is a matter of preparation meeting opportunity."*

During my own career and throughout my research of successful executives, I have found that preparation, opportunity, and luck, is often responsible for the success of many. When these three components come together, success is imminent. Anyone who has worked with me will often hear me say:

"Prepare for the opportunity, in which you may just be lucky enough to be at the right time and place to take advantage of it."

Let's talk about these ingredients a little further.

SUPER INGREDIENT#1: **PREPARATION**

"What I learned from working in restaurants is that preparation is everything." -Jocelyn

If you look at the prep work in a busy restaurant, you will see that much of the work occurs before opening. All the veggies are cut, ice is stocked, garnishes are ready, spices are mixed and sauces are prepared. Being adequately prepared in the restaurant business is critical and is the difference between one that runs like a well-oiled machine and one that is chaotic. In restaurants, preparation is the key to efficiency.

Preparation is also the key to efficiency when it comes to your career. Adequate preparation can save you from rework, waste and disappointments. Research shows that most successful people, whether in business, corporate, entertainment, sports and any other arena, start with extreme preparation. When it comes to success, the more successful one is, the more prepared they tend to be. Most successful people will tell you that they have been preparing for success most of their lives.

The interesting thing about success is that when you're looking at someone who is successful, what you see is that person in his or her current successful state. However, if you could go back in time, you would see that they were preparing for their future success in many different ways. A wonderful example of how preparation leads to great success is the success story of Bill Gates, chairman of Microsoft.

THE SUCCESS STORY OF BILL GATES

Bill Gates started programming computers at the age of thirteen, in eighth grade at an exclusive preparatory school in Seattle, Washington. Gates had such a strong interest in the inner workings of the computer, that he was excused from his math classes to pursue this interest. How's that for preparing for a future in the software business? Gates is known for having written his first computer program on that same school's computer.

Gates also ran a small business as a young teenager with his childhood friend, Paul Allen. That business, named Traf-O-Data, sold one of its computers to the city of Seattle. He designed a software program to count city traffic. Gates was seventeen years old at the time. Gates prepared by spending upwards of ten hours a day working at the computer.

Another good example of the role preparation plays in lives of successful people is that of actor, George Clooney. George Clooney is one of Hollywood's most formidable renaissance men. His father Nick Clooney, a broadcast journalist, hosted a TV talk show and he often invited five-year-old George onto the set. Young George would hang around often participating in shows, where he proved to be a crowd favorite. I was amazed when I discovered that he had been acting in minor roles and honing his craft from as early as 1978.

According to Wikipedia, after a decade spent toiling on television series mostly in minor roles, he catapulted to stardom with his portrayal of a charming but troubled pediatrician, Doug Ross on the television show, ER, in 1994. Clooney had several setbacks during his preparation of stardom, including coming back from a few movie failures before becoming a true success. Clooney understood the benefit of preparation.

Preparation comes in many forms and is specific to your career or business goals. For many professional fields, a college education is a prerequisite. You will never be a lawyer without having gone to law school. Preparation is about obtaining the required education, certification, and/or training. Actually very successful people tend to prepare like crazy. If you know of anyone who is very successful, I bet you will find that they handle themselves as if they are training for the Olympics. Like Thomas Edison once said,

"Genius is one percent inspiration and, ninety-nine percent perspiration."

Successful people are often goal-directed and an important goal is to be prepared when opportunity knocks. They know that adequate preparation is the first-class ticket to career advancement.

SUPER INGREDIENT #2: **OPPORTUNITY**

"No matter how much you prepare, it's getting access to opportunities that makes the difference." -Jocelyn

Access to opportunities is the next super ingredient common to successful people. Being around the right people at the right time is critical. Opportunity is about being at the right place. (Luck is being there at the right time.) We all know that some people obtain this access of 'being there' through family and friend connections and the wonderful networks that having that accessibility provides. They are the fortunate ones and consequently have a head start over others. Others however, have to make these connections themselves. Not having ready access to influential people will require you to work harder to obtain it. However, it is worth the effort.

In the world of business, it is "who you know" that matters, especially when it comes to increasing access to opportunities. Therefore, making the right strategic connections is of the utmost importance. However, just having the right connections won't do a thing for you if you are not prepared to take advantage of the opportunities when they present themselves.

Many women find making connections challenging. Most of us cringe when we think of networking and downright hate it in many cases. "Who has the time to network?" is often a question I hear my clients say. As women, we also struggle trying to figure out who should be in our networking circle and how to approach them. I will discuss how to build an effective networking strategy in the chapter on supportive networks.

SUPER INGREDIENT #3: **LUCK**

" Some people just seem to have a monopoly on good luck! Being in the right place and time pays off big time!" -Jocelyn

Our cultural views of luck may vary. Some may view luck as a matter of random chance. Others may attribute luck as a means of faith and superstition. However, luck is an important factor in many successful careers. According to Webster's definition, luck is a force that brings good fortune or adversity and is the events or circumstances that operate for or against an individual.

Contemporary authors, who have written on the subject, believe that luck is an important factor in many aspects of our society. They state that luck or fortuity, is either good or bad fortune. They see luck as being caused by accident or chance. Although it cannot be proven that luck actually exists, most people will tell you that they have some sense that it does. Many believe that it is a real phenomenon and that they have experienced it in some form.

It is thought that a belief in luck produces for the believer, positive perspectives. People who believe in the concept of good luck are more optimistic, more satisfied with their lives and have better moods. Also, many believe that they seem to draw good luck towards them. Lucky people often see the glass as half full rather than half empty.

Often when I talk about the importance of luck, many people either chuckle and get it, or feel hopeless, believing that their luck will never come. Some struggle with the unscientific concept of luck. However, regardless of your feelings and comfort level, my research, along with the research of others, confirms that when it comes to success, most successful people were simply lucky to have been in the right place, at the right time to take advantage of a great opportunity. Sometimes things are just meant to be, and if you're lucky, you will be prepared to take advantage of some great opportunities.

Although luck is a critical ingredient, don't make the common mistake I see many make. The mistake is believing that luck alone is the key to success. Although many of us believe that luck is the reason that someone becomes successful; people's success rarely rests on luck alone. It is luck along with adequate preparation that is key to most success stories.

When you examine the multi layers of a career from any one of the successful people you admire, you will find that they spent many years preparing for their lucky opportunity. It is actually the preparation not the luck, which allowed them to take advantage of the opportunity.

A GRILLED CHEESE SANDWICH STORY

A woman I know was offered a great opportunity to become a trainer for a nationally known company. This position would allow her to travel the world and do what she loved.

Her lucky opportunity came while she was speaking at a women's convention. Public speaking and professional training was something she had been doing for several years at the time. At a break, she was approached by a recruiter and asked if she would be interested in a training position.

As it turned out, the recruiter had overheard her presentation while walking past the training room. She was struck with the way the woman held the group's attention and how well she used both humor and tone of voice to keep the group's focus.

They agreed to meet for breakfast the next morning. After breakfast, she walked out of the restaurant with a verbal six-figure job offer. How is that for preparation, opportunity and luck?

The above story illustrates how all three super ingredients worked in her favor. Because she had been speaking publically for over a decade, she was prepared. The women's conference provided the opportunity to be seen and heard by someone who had an interest in what she did. If she had not been given the opportunity to train at the conference, she would not have been in the right place at the right time when luck came her way.

Several great examples of these three super ingredients coming together is captured in the article, "What Was Your Biggest Break?" found in the February 2011 edition of *O Magazine*. In this article, successful public personalities such as Meredith Vieira formally of the *Today Show*, Suze Orman, Holly Robinson Peete and Ellen DeGeneres talk about their lucky breaks.

Meredtih Vieira's big break came when she was lucky to get a bad perm. Because she wore a hat, (to hide her hair disaster), she was put on outdoor assignments. These outdoor assignments got her visibility on television, thus putting her on the map. Her success grew from there.

Suze Orman's big break came when she was lucky to lose all of her money. To get back on her feet, she prepared herself to understand finance and investing. This preparation gave her the opportunity to go to Merrill Lynch's training program, later becoming an executive there as well. Her success grew from there.

Holly Robinson Peete's big break came from someone giving her a chance. After auditioning for the part in *21 Jump Street*, the producers happen to hear her horrible screeching brakes on her broken down Honda. Feeling sorry for her, they gave her a break and she got the part. Her success grew from there.

Barbara Walters' big break came when the then "Today Girl," Maureen O'Sullivan, couldn't handle the demands of the *Today Show*. Therefore, Barbara, a writer at the time, was a cheap replacement. Only hired for a 13-week assignment, she ended up being there for 13 years. Her success grew from there.

Ellen DeGeneres' big break came from getting booked on *The Tonight Show* with Johnny Carson and being lucky enough to be the first female comedian to be asked over to his coach. This gave her exposure. Her success grew from there.

The big breaks mentioned above are great examples of lucky situations that opened the door for success. However, each one of the success stories required the woman to be prepared, or have the will to prepare for their roles. Therefore, luck is no match for preparation. Nothing will substitute for preparation. I love the statement from Arnold Palmer after responding to a fan's comment on his lucky swing. Palmer's statement was, *"The more I practice, the luckier I get."* You must practice and be prepared. Then when luck comes your way, you can take advantage of it.

Having looked at preparation, opportunity and luck and their role in succuss, we must also examine a number of other ingredients that come together to assist us in being successful. While the *"Super Ingredients"* are important, the other ingedients that contribute to career success are considerd "Sure-fire Ingredients." Now, let's get into the meat of career success.

The Sure-fire Ingredients

Building Your Sandwich
Preparing for the opportunities coming your way.

1. Self-Confidence
2. Leveraged Talents
3. Golden Reputation
4. Effective Self-promotion
5. Supportive Networks
6. Diverse Mentors & Sponsors
7. Positive Relationships
8. Exceptional Communication Skills
9. Strategy and Execution
10. Influence Over Others

What's In Your Sandwich?

Sure-fire Ingredient #1
A Bunch of Self-Confidence

"You don't need to see yourself as 'better' than others. You just need to see yourself as 'just as good.'" -Jocelyn

EXECUTIVE CHEF

Bob Fish | President & CEO, Biggby Coffee

A Candid Discussion on Self Confidence with Bob Fish, President & CEO, Biggby Coffee

"Confidence doesn't mean bullying, overpowering or dominating a room. It s just a sense that you are comfortable in the environment that you are in at that moment in time. It is how you hold your shoulders, how high you hold your chin, how you look people in the eye; it is how you present yourself to the public

as you interact with them. That presentation has a large impact in terms of how people perceive how you are doing." – Bob Fish

The best cup of coffee I ever had was on the day I met with Bob Fish, aka, Biggby Bob. Although he is an extremely successful entrepreneur poised to be the Midwest king of gourmet coffee, Bob is a very modest man. His generous and engaging spirit puts one at ease in his presence.

I originally reached out to Bob after watching him speak on Public Television. At the time, Bob was sharing the core values by which he runs his company. His approach on confidence caught my attention. Via email, I asked Bob for an opportunity to discuss his perspective on confidence. Since building confidence is the foundation of what I do, I was interested in learning more about how he viewed confidence in terms of his personal and business success. Within two hours, I received a response back from him agreeing to meet.

Bob and I met at the Biggby in downtown Birmingham, Michigan. Bob managed to squeeze me in his schedule while in the area between meetings. During our conversation, Bob shared great insights on the importance of self-confidence while building a successful career and business. His rich wisdom and understated savvy was captivating and honest.

BOB'S CAREER JOURNEY

Bob was born in Germany, and is the son of a German mother and American father. During most of his childhood, he lived in Europe; living in Germany, France and England. His father worked for Ford Motor Company, a job that had overseas assignments that lasted up to four years at a time. Although they lived in Europe for extended periods, their home base was Metro Detroit.

According to Bob, this overseas experience allowed him the privilege to grow up with a wide-world perspective. He was fortunate to see the world through a different lens from an early age. This contributed to his ability to look at things from different perspectives.

Bob came back to the states to go to college in 1981. He attended Michigan State University (MSU) in Lansing, Michigan. After graduating from the American School in London (a K-12 school with approximately 200 students), going to MSU was overwhelming at first. Seeing the campus for the first time at age 17 years old, without ever visiting the campus before enrolling, was a culture shock.

In college, his original major was engineering. However, after his first engineering class, he knew that it was not for him. He didn't feel that he belonged with the other students. He changed majors a few times, going from engineering, to no-preference, to a business major. Eventually, he graduated with a major in hospitality.

Bob described himself as *"not a very good student from a GPA perspective."* He was a hard worker and put his own self through school working as a prep cook at a local family-style restaurant. Having to work through school, it took him eight years to complete a four-year degree program. His typical day at that time started with going to the restaurant early in the morning to cut potatoes, onions, and make soup. For eight years, he was on a cycle of working for a bit, going to school for a bit, and so on. Finally, after eight years, he graduated.

By the time he graduated from MSU, he was running the restaurant where he worked. The owners eventually asked him to help them grow the business. Bob agreed to assist them with the promise that the owners would help him own his own restaurant. The deal resulted in going from one to four restaurants, with Bob owning the third one.

With a co-loan from the original owners, Bob opened his first restaurant in 1991. The family restaurant was a success, bringing in $1.6 million *"selling just pancakes and eggs and without selling alcohol,"* according to Bob. He sold the restaurant two years later.

The day after selling the restaurant, Bob jumped in his car and took off on a road trip. After spending years working 16-hour days and going to school, he needed to get away. He had a desire to broaden his view and determine his next move. According to Bob, *"I had some ideas in my head and shook them out during this road trip. I made it all the way from Lansing, Michigan to Brownsville, Texas."*

By the time he made it to Texas, he had settled on his next business idea. He wanted to sell specialty coffees. This realization pointed him to Seattle, Washington, where he headed next. He spent four months hanging out with *"micro roasters who were at the beginning of the 'coffee wave.'"* This was in 1995.

Needing money for his new business venture, he had to learn how to write a business plan. The concept of selling coffee as a business model was a hard sell. After several rejections, he finally secured a bank loan after trying nine times. Bob compared getting a loan to interviewing for a job.

"Maybe the first interview doesn't go so well, but after your ninth one, you get the hang of it and become more confident. This is where practice makes perfect."

Bob began his coffee business in East Lansing, Michigan, the most unlikely place to start a specialty coffee shop. At the time, the environment and economy was tough for such a business. The first shop opened on March 15, 1995. At that time, Bob described himself as "a shopkeeper." He made the coffee, steamed the milk and rang up the cash register. The first six months were difficult. The majority of what he learned and the business values he still follows today came from his experience in the first six-eighteen months of opening. During that time, he used all of his savings, maxed out all of his credit cards, and sold all of his cars.

"A great example of choosing to be confident was showing up every day with a smile and convincing people that everything was going well. That was when faith really came in handy." said Bob.

However, 18 months after opening, the location was making $1 million without spending one dollar on marketing.

According to Bob, the 3 D's (*desire, dedication and determination*) played a major role in his success. In two years, he opened a second store. Soon people were approaching him on how they could open their own store. Mary Ellen Sheets, owner of *Two Men and a Truck,* helped him understand the franchising business. She shared her experience and lessons learned about franchising. According to Bob, she gave him the gift of confidence that he could do it.

"When you have questions, go to the people who you think have the answers." What he found was that most people will take the time to share what they know. In 1999, he sold his first two franchise units. At the time of my interview with Bob, Biggby was at 130 units with plans to have 159 by the end of 2011—what he calls a "fair accomplishment." He spends little time looking backwards, instead he only looks forward.

Biggby's cultural values are: "Be Happy, Have Fun, Make Friends, Love People and Drink Great Coffee."

BOB'S PERSPECTIVE ON CONFIDENCE
(in his words)

When it comes to confidence, I seldom talk about it without the two companions, faith and courage. I don't believe confidence is enough without the other two.

Faith is important. Faith is what helps bring you that degree of confidence. Faith can be something that is external, like religion, or it can be spiritually inside.

In a small business, and entreprencurial endeavors, one needs faith in order to survive difficult moments in time.

Everyone has difficult times. If one does not, maybe they are not trying hard enough or they are the smartest person on earth. There are difficult times in careers as well. Early in careers or new roles, there are not many people there to support you. The bench is not deep. Also if your ideas are different than the norm, that is even more true. Then when times get difficult and you look behind you, there is nobody there. At that moment in time, you have to rely on faith in order to get you through it.

Faith influences your confidence. If you don't have faith in what you are doing, you will feel alone and scared. This influences your confidence because when you are alone in your thoughts and struggles, without faith, your confidence is shattered. This is what makes confidence and faith interdependent.

Courage is linked into confidence differently. Courage is doing something you are afraid of anyway. Just like a soldier in the army. They put themselves in harm's way. They may be killed or wounded, but they go out and fight anyway. That is courage.

Sometimes we describe our fear as risk, and we have internal fears that plague us as well. It takes courage to keep moving forward even when we are afraid. Courage is like asking for money when you know that you may be rejected. Courage is looking yourself in the eye and being honest about your limitations and fears. Courage allows you to overcome that.

Confidence does not happen in isolation. Confidence is a choice. In order to have that confidence, you have to examine your faith and you have to examine your courage and determine whether you are willing to put yourself in a situation that is unsafe to you. Doubt is a driving force for excellence and having the ability to excel. Even stage actors have panic attacks prior to going on stage.

The lack of confidence is rampart in business. Confidence helped Biggby survive because we took a different approach to specialty coffee. We decided to not be exclusive or intimidating. This is contrary to other coffee shops. Everyone else did what every else does. We had the confidence to be different.

To boost your confidence, you must be willing to do a self-examination. Conduct an inventory of who you are. Know where you are lacking to be truly successful. Once you understand your limitations, you can choose to improve them, or find someone else who can help you like a coach. You need to conquer your weak points or supplement them with someone else's expertise.

Uncovering who you are, that is what allows you to move forward. Until you unpeel who you are, you are chasing your demons left and right. This can be distracting. When it comes to confidence, ownership is critical. You must be the owner of your actions. You are responsible for where you want to go.

The erosion of confidence is fear. That is why you cannot ignore courage. Fear is the reflection of the unknown.

In order to master confidence, one must:

Practice: *It is important in building confidence. Dress rehearsals work wonders.*
Open yourself to criticism: *It is a pathway to improvement.*
Be vulnerable: *It helps conquer confidence.*

BOB'S OTHER LESSONS LEARNED AND ADVICE

When making choices, I often thought, "If you could write your obituary today, what would you want it to say?" When I thought of my own obituary, I wanted to be well respected in the community, financially independent and have the freedom to travel and be wherever I wanted to be.

None of what you do is accidental. You must decide to do it. Wishing, dreaming, coveting is not enough. Overcoming your fear, while understanding the amount of dedication it takes to execute is important. Know that dedication and success always comes with sacrifice.

THE POWER OF CONFIDENCE IN YOURSELF

Over the years, I've learned that the journey to success is often a bumpy ride. The path to the top is not always clear and many times the route is confusing. Confidence is the glue that will hold you together on this journey of ups and downs. Confidence also gives you the resiliency that allows you to move forward in tough times. It provides the courage to take risks and the persona that earns respect-- all of which are critical to career success.

Many women need to either develop self-confidence or improve upon what they already have. That is not to say the men don't suffer from a lack of confidence, many of them do as well. Women however, tend to be more self-critical and fall under unique scrutiny through double standards. Due to this, our self-confidence is constantly being challenged.

When you exhibit self-confidence, you appear more credible than someone who does not. Confidence will help you to be taken seriously. Confidence also increases assertiveness, which is important in career advancement. It takes assertiveness to ask for the money you deserve, or for a promotion and credit for a job well done.

LET CONFIDENCE BE YOUR BREAD

"Any good sandwich starts with good bread. When it comes to your career, confidence is your bread." –Jocelyn

Let's look to the sandwich analogy for a moment. When you set out to make a sandwich, I am sure many of you would agree that selecting the right kind of bread is critical. In fact, many chefs would say that the sandwich is only as good as the bread in which it is made. Therefore, the bread is the foundation of the sandwich in which everything else is built. The same is true for confidence. Confidence is the bread of your career strategy. It is on confidence that everything else is built.

When selecting the right bread for your sandwich, your selection is contingent on the kind of sandwich you're building. For instance, you would never pick a small piece of fluffy white bread and try to build a big, stacked, corn beef sandwich on it, would you? The sandwich would just fall apart. The bread has to be able to stand up to the sandwich. The same is true with your career. The amount of confidence you need is related to the type of career you are building. The higher you go on the career ladder, or in business, the more confidence you will need.

When it comes to building a strong foundation, many women, when asked, would say that they have a rock solid foundation. If they have a few years of work under their belt, they are even more likely to feel this way. However, more times than not, most women have misconceptions about what constitutes as a solid foundation and many of us are building careers on shaky ground. Shaky foundations cause buildings to topple over. I have seen career mishaps do the same.

"Success in early careers can lead to a false sense of confidence. Many of us are promoted prematurely, without strong foundations of confidence. When we hit bumps, our careers get shaky and derail at times." -Jocelyn

Many people build their foundations in their early careers. It is important to understand that when we are in this phase, we are often selfishly motivated. Some people get offended when I say this. So, let me explain what I mean...

When we first enter the professional arena, we tend to be focused on how much money we'll be making, or how we can advance within the company, and what wonderful perks we'll receive. This approach causes us to be short- sighted. We are unable to see the forest for the trees. Dazzled by rapid advancement, we feel powerful when we are tapped and fast-tracked.

Because we are easily persuaded in early careers, many are prematurely promoted during this phase. When we show strong motivation, our leaders often view us as having the right talent to be promoted or given more responsibilities. Many eager professionals are promoted without a properly built foundation. This has the potential to create failure in early careers.

Failures in early careers can damage the reputation of young professionals. Instead of working on sure-fire objectives of this critical phase, many end up focusing on salvaging a declining reputation. When one has early failures in their career, it has a detrimental effect on their confidence. And building one's confidence is the key objective for building a strong foundation.

A FOUNDATION PITFALL

A common misconception women make is believing that the more education and experience they have, the stronger their foundation. This can't be farther from the truth. No matter how much education and experience you have, you will find that your career will plateau if you neglect to incorporate the foundation ingredient of confidence into your career strategy.

WHAT CONFIDENCE IS AND WHAT IT IS NOT

There is an inherent difference between being self-confident and being arrogant. When it comes to confidence, most women tell me that they are reluctant to "act too confident" because they don't want to come off as arrogant. Being arrogant is not a perception most women want to earn. In fact, we hate arrogance. Knowing the difference is important, as it is easy to confuse the two. In my opinion, the main difference between confidence and arrogance is:

Confidence is about "you." When you are "confident," you believe in yourself, and feel assured that your results will be positive.

Arrogance on the other hand, is about how you feel about yourself compared to others.

Arrogant people believe that they are better than others and they like everyone to know it.

I have a great story that demonstrates the difference between confidence and arrogance ...

A 'HAM' SANDWICH STORY

A friend of mine, Diane, had the opportunity to work with a small group of people to promote a cause that was near and dear to her heart. At the first meeting, they were asked to share what they had that they could bring to the cause.

Several members raised their hands and stated things like; 'I write well,' 'I can create a web site,' 'I can type,' 'I'm an accountant,' 'I have meeting space at work,' and things of that sort.

All of a sudden, a very well dressed man stood up and walked to the front of the room. He stood there and waited until he had their full attention. Once all eyes were on him, he proceeded to tell the group that he was an established businessman who made a great deal of money.

He said, "In fact, if I told you just how much money I make, you wouldn't believe me."
He was a tall man who obviously was not afraid of speaking in front of groups and enjoyed gaining the command of a room.

He went on to tell them things about his education, his business, his lifestyle, his children, talking nonstop for many minutes. He told the group that one of his many talents was making people dig deep into their pockets and give, and give until it hurt. That, he said, would be his contribution to the group.

He concluded by saying he could bring in money from well over fifty to sixty other highly influential people whom he knew personally. The group went wild with excitement, clapping their hands and cheering his promise of financial aid to the cause. Needless to say, the meeting ended on a high note. Interestingly enough, less than two weeks after his offer to help raise large sums of cash, his picture was plastered all over the front page of the local newspaper. He had been arrested for swindling many people out of huge sums of money, and he was also bankrupt!

My friend, Diane, mistakenly saw his takeover of the meeting as a show of confidence. However, his behavior was a sure sign of arrogance. The soon to be imprisoned businessman showed his arrogance and a healthy dose of superiority over all those in attendance. What he, in fact, did was attempt to charm the audience into seeing him as he wanted to be seen; a great success. His need to have the group admire him and his larger than life accomplishments was certainly arrogance and not a shred of confidence.

OBTAINING CONFIDENCE

Confidence is a feeling of self-assurance. It's having faith in your personal resources such as your ability, judgment and talent. Rosabeth Moss Kanter in her book, **Confidence** (2006) states, *"Confidence consists of positive expectations for favorable outcomes."* According to Kanter, confidence underlies the performance of individuals, teams, businesses, schools, economies and nations. Kanter also writes,

"Confidence grows from knowing one's strengths and working to improve them, investing in other people, and achieving small wins by tackling

challenges with a positive outlook. Confidence is the bridge connecting expectations and performance, investment and results."

Being prepared is a great way to maintaining and enhancing your confidence. Preparation will allow you to feel confident within any setting. So always do your homework.

AN IMPORTANT KEY TO CONFIDENCE IS PICKING THE RIGHT JOBS

One way to gaining confidence is to set yourself up for wins and successes. The more wins you receive, the more confidence you develop. This is especially important in early careers when you are building your foundation. It is imperative, that you select the right jobs for your skills, knowledge and abilities. In the early stages of your career, picking jobs that suit your talents and personality is important. To put it in simple terms, if you are a people person, pick a job that will allow you to work with people. If you are a numbers person, pick a job that will allow you to crunch the numbers. The point is to select jobs that you know will highlight your talents. Your early position(s) should be carefully selected to ensure that the best of you comes shining through.

Setting yourself up for wins and successes is also dependant on selecting the right working environment compatible with your personality. Working in the wrong environment can make you unhappy and resentful.

Therefore, it is imperative to do research on the company, your future supervisor and the team or department dynamics. Many times I've seen how joining the wrong team, company or boss, can kill the spirit of the most talented people. Before accepting a position, find out as much information as possible before joining. If the job doesn't fit you, don't torce it.

You can also improve upon your confidence even if you have been working in your chosen field for many years. Selecting the right projects and keeping your skills current can help to maintain your confidence.

YOUR PERSONAL APPEARANCE IMPACTS YOUR SELF-CONFIDENCE

For women, feeling good about how we look contributes significantly in how confident we feel. If we are uncomfortable about our personal appearance, it comes across through our body language and causes us to feel insecure. All of these dimensions affect how we portray our confidence to others.

When my clients are unhappy about their appearance, I tell them that they have two options:

1. **Do something about it, or**
2. **Embrace it and work with it.**

If you don't like the way you look, it is important to do something about it, or embrace and make the best of it. Start you fitness routine to get in shape if that is your problem. Spruce up your wardrobe; get help from sales associates in your local department store. You will be amazed at what a few accessories can do for a wardrobe makeover. A new haircut can do wonders as well. However, if you are not going to change your appearance, change how you think about yourself. Appreciate and focus on your positive attributes and if possible, flaunt them. When you feel good about yourself, it shows. It's liberating and you will find that you are more confident to meet your challenges.

SPEAKING WITH CONFIDENCE

Speaking with confidence is also critical to career success. If public speaking is not one of your strong points, you can almost bet your life savings that you are not going to climb very far within the organization. An inability to speak well in a public forum could derail your career climb. Don't let the inability to speak with confidence become a barrier to your career advancement.

The most successful people are those who can effectively communicate with other people either one-on-one or in groups, both, large or small. You will increase your confidence dramatically if you obtain professional training in communication skills and practice speaking in public as often as you can. We will discuss more on communication in the chapter on *Effective Communication*.

Extra Toppings to Enhance Your Sandwich

◎ Practice positive self-talk

◎ Come prepared and practice

◎ Be honest about your limitations

◎ Visualize a successful future

◎ Pick the right jobs, teams and bosses

chapter five

Sure-fire Ingredient #2 Leveraged Talents

"Once your talents are focused and developed, they can be the strengths that propel you forward." -Jocelyn

EXECUTIVE CHEF

Kimberly Rath, President | Talent Plus

An Honest Discussion on Leveraged Talent With Kimberly Rath, President, Talent Plus

"What would the world be like if everybody did what they were good at and enjoyed?"
-Dr. William E. Hall
(One of the Founders of Talent Plus)

I had the pleasure of working with Kimberly Rath when I held the position of vice president of talent and workforce strategies, for Henry

Ford West Bloomfield Hospital (HFWBH), West Bloomfield, Michigan.

HFWBH is the largest Michigan hospital project meeting national green-building standards.

Besides reducing noise, waste and energy consumption, the hospital, which opened in March 2009, was also voted the second most beautiful hospital in the country by Soliant Health's Top 20 Most Beautiful Hospital List.

In 2007, I was leading talent strategies for the hospital . We partnered with Kimberly's company, Talent Plus, to develop a process for selecting and developing top talent. Kimberly and her team, along with my leadership, collaborated to build a talent-based organization for Henry Ford Health System's new hospital.

Early in our partnership, I visited Kimberly at the Talent Plus headquarters in Lincoln, Nebraska. From the moment I walked in the building, I knew I was in a talent-based organization. They were "walking the talk" and I was sold. When they talked about leveraging and developing talent, they knew what they were talking about and it showed.

Talent Plus' corporate building is very modern, with many windows. The light flows through the entire building just like the talent. The open and airy space made me feel free and I understood how the physical environment promoted creativity and innovation.

The warm greetings I received as I walked through made me feel at home. It was evident that each person liked their job and it came natural to them. From what I would call the receptionist (I say that because at Talent Plus, no one has job titles), to their specialists, people seemed happy to serve.

Another interesting thing I found while visiting, was that Talent Plus encourages the hiring of family and friends. It amazed me to see husbands and wives working together--a practice often discouraged at most organizations. In fact, Talent Plus actively recruits spouses as a way to create an engaging culture. This effort also contributes to healthy relationships. Couples are able to carpool, understand job demands and spend more time together.

The Talent Plus team was phenomenal. Their credibility was earned with me when I could see that in their own selection process, they had selected the right talent for the right roles. The people I worked with were perfectly fitted for his or her position and for the company's culture. Together we developed talent assessment selection tools and a talent-based coaching/ development process that set the groundwork and infrastructure for one of the nation's most innovative hospitals.

Today, Henry Ford West Bloomfield Hospital is a known leader in innovation, talent retention and customer satisfaction.

KIMBERLY'S CAREER JOURNEY

Kimberly started her career in retail at 16 years old wrapping gifts for the holidays. Therefore, her first professional experience was in service. She stated that this experience helped her understand that she enjoyed servicing others, making memorable experiences and making something special for someone else. Working since high school, Kimberly believes she is hardwired for service and hard work. Those are her talents.

Kimberly has also possessed a keen interest in the historical study of people. She has a great affinity for children and understanding what makes them tick. Therefore, she studied elementary education at the University of Nebraska-Lincoln. While at the University, she served as a counselor in the Nebraska Human Resources Research Institute (SRI)– a program that was started by one of Talent Plus' founders, Dr. William E. Hall in the 1950s.

Following college, Kimberly worked at SRI as a leadership consultant. Her focus was to help organizations identify what tools to use to meet their talent goals. SRI was eventually purchased by Gallup where she worked for several years until Dr. Hall and his wife founded Talent Plus with Sandy Maxwell, Kimberly's husband, Doug Rath and Kimberly in 1989.

Talent Plus works with several organizations, helping to support their talent selection initiatives. With over 200 clients across the globe – many who have been recognized as leaders in their industry and others have been designated as "Great Places to Work," Talent Plus has played a major role in their talent management.

Organizations such as The Ritz-Carlton Hotel Company (the only hospitality company to have twice won the U.S. Department of Commerce Malcolm Baldrige National Quality Award), the Estée Lauder Companies, Mercedes-Benz USA, DFS, Dr Pepper Snapple Group, Cancer Treatment Centers of America, UCLA Health System, Microsoft, Henry Ford West Bloomfield Hospital and Shangri-La Hotels and Resorts all have partnered with Talent Plus to build talent-based organizations.

Today, Talent Plus has offices in Lincoln, Nebraska, Singapore and Bogota, Colombia. Kimberly travels the globe speaking to leadership groups on talent selection and development. Her journey also includes raising her children. She enjoys watching their choices and pursuits as young adults and how these choices fit their talent.

Kimberly is committed to her community and therefore serves on various community boards. Boards such as Nelnet, Inc.'s where she served as the Education Chair for Young Presidents' Organization (YPO), allows her to give back. She is also a passionate advocate for CARE and a member of Cather Circle (Nebraska Alumni Association's mentoring/networking organization) and served as a member of the Lincoln City County Child Care Advisory Board and the Nebraska Center for Entrepreneurship (helping it gain recognition as the No. 1 Undergraduate Entrepreneurship Education Program).

KIMBERLY'S PERSPECTIVE ON
LEVERAGED TALENTS *(in her words)*

In my opinion, a talent:

◎ *Is a natural ability not acquired through effort, education or experience.*
◎ *Results in spontaneous behavior on the part of the individual.*
◎ *Results in intrinsic satisfaction when the individual's talent is being maximized.*
◎ *Can be measured so behavior can be predicted and matched with the correct job or skill.*
◎ *Can be coached to achieve excellence through individual investment.*

We think about talent in terms of our growth formula:
(Talent + Fit) x Investment = Growth

We believe that talent is innate and that it is skills that can be learned. You can improve and refine the talents you have, but you can't create them. When individuals focus on what they are good at, studies show that individuals can get even better. In opposition to this, individuals who focus on their weaknesses may make some small improvements, but the growth is never going to be as vast as those who focus on their talent.

In the workplace, managers hire individuals because of what they bring to the table and in some organizations spend that individual's career life cycle – attempting to "fix" all of the things they didn't select this person for. Instead, we work with talent-based cultures where they are focusing on a varsity vs. a recreational mindset. Think about when you played a sport growing up. At first, you probably played on a league or team that was recreational where everyone had the opportunity to play. As you grew up, you may have focused on a varsity team where the coach thought strategically about which player played in which situation of a game. Some players are ones you send in because they are faster or shoot better or they may have a special skill set such as a particular type of pitch or a particular type of play.

Using this metaphor of varsity vs. recreational, talent-based organizations select their players for their talent, pay particular attention to the role they will be filling and ensure that their manager/coach understands those talents and how they work in the organization. The manager/coach sets clear expectations, provides developmental coaching and sees a succession plan for the future.

Organizations that select talent find that individuals in the right role and coached in a way that develops this talent, increase productivity. In turn, that talent increases their ROI, customer satisfaction, employee engagement and they find that there are industry specific metrics that improve as well, – i.e. in health care – lower infection rates, decreased morbidity rates, shorter length of stay, etc.

Companies who partner with Talent Plus, come to us really for two higher arching reasons. One path is they have a business problem they are trying to solve and through our solutions aimed at front line, middle management, senior leaders – we can assist them. These might be issues of retention, development, succession planning, opening a new location, turnover, etc.

The other path is when a senior leader sees an opportunity to take their business to the next level. They are on top of their niche and they are high performing cultures. However, they know that in a quest for constant improvement, the next step is through their people. All of these paths involve talent-based solutions aimed at their most important commodity in their business-- their people.

What we at Talent Plus do really better than anyone in the marketplace is deliver an understanding of peoples' hardwiring. We have found that our strong selection tools help select individuals who are top performers, individuals who can anticipate the needs of their customers and deliver outstanding customer service and/or sales.

Most importantly, we ascribe to the philosophy of one our founders, Dr. William E. Hall. The philosophy is around the question, "What would the world be like if everybody did what they were good at and enjoyed?"

The name of the company, "Talent Plus" is based on the focus of understanding the potentiality someone brings to the workforce or their "talent." The "plus" is about relationships. The only way someone can understand someone's talents, develop that talent, and provide meaningful rewards, comes from the relationship that a manager creates with an individual on their team and the team as a whole.

Talent Plus is interested in individual potentiality and when leveraged, the power it has on an organization and its culture.

HOW CAN INDIVIDUALS LEVERAGE THEIR TALENT TO ADVANCE THEIR CAREERS?

Having an understanding of your own talent and where your strengths lie is best described in what we talk about when we say people are in flow. In flow is like, when time passes by so quickly that you hardly realize how much time you've spent on something. These are the moments when you have the opportunity to do work that you are good at and you enjoy.

Appreciating what people are good at and enjoy is an opportunity for organizations to look at nontraditional advancement opportunities. Some individuals are currently in the right position for their talent. To advance them under a traditional career ladder may not make sense. They may not have the talent for that next rung. At Talent Plus, we think it makes better sense for individuals to be rewarded in the positions that make sense for them and that career ladders need to be re-defined. Organizations really need to look at what defines advancement in order to retain top talent.

When organizations leverage their talent, they are better able to be nimble, resourceful and be forward facing. We have seen this in our clients coming out of this recent economic downturn. Talent Plus clients are experiencing great growth this year. When you have hardwired your organization with individuals who are optimistic, resilient, resourceful and forward thinking, you have the opportunity to bounce back sooner when the economy rebounds.

Our tools are ethnicity, gender and age blind. So I don't think about things in terms of male and female connotations. Today, I think our clients are looking at talent in an androgynous way. In fact, as organizations move forward, a platform of talent has provided opportunities for individuals who might not have been selected in a traditional way. Our interviews and assessments provide companies an opportunity to look at talent, with age, experience and ethnicity stripped away and these organizations are probably much further ahead in looking at diversity of their selections because they are focused solely on talent.

One of the things that I continue to be very interested in is in the study of young people. The work that we do with adults today would rapidly accelerate had these individuals had this understanding at a younger age. We work with young people today through our young leaders academy and through several institutions of higher learning as well as through some school systems.

I have a real passion for where this collaboration may take our communities. If everyone focused on talent from a young age and instructors were selected for their talent as teachers, they would have a better understanding of each student in the classroom. And, the bonus would be that parents would have a better understanding of their children's talents as well. I get very excited about this potential reinvestment principle.

A CHICKEN SALAD SANDWICH STORY

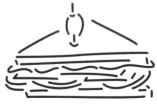

"Be who you is, 'cause if you be who you ain't, you ain't who you is."

My sister, Angela, wrote that quote across her bedroom wall as a teenager. Although that was many years ago, I never forgot it.

As grammatically incorrect as it sounds, to "be

who you is," is a profound statement. Most of us are constantly being told to change and be "who we ain't." We are rarely told to "be who we is," often fighting our natural tendencies.

That statement made such an impact on me, I wrote it in my yearbook as my mantra and advice to the senior high school class. Even equipped with my mantra, it still took me years to discover "who I was" in the corporate world. I went through phases of trying to be what I thought I should be, based on what types of behaviors I assumed would get me to the top.

One of the styles I sought was to be "Ms. Tough." I used to envy women who didn't take any mess. They demanded respect and appeared to gain it. These "tough women" went through their careers not really caring about individual feelings. If you wanted to succeed on their team, you either got on board, or got out.

Finding out what makes people tick always energized me. I never saw weaknesses in people, but just differences in styles, talents, and approaches. I believed that my role as a leader was to bring out the best in everyone. However, that approach was seldom rewarded in the corporate world. Many leaders tried to coach me into being more like "Ms. Tough." I was encouraged to be harder on people, address their weaknesses, and let them know who the boss was.

Although this tough approach was not working for me, I found it difficult to ignore the coaching of my superiors. Soon, I found myself on a quest to become "Ms Tough." I read every book on assertiveness, etc. My mission was to adopt a more "stern" edge and I took on that mission with a vengeance.

Then one day after becoming frustrated because I wasn't making progress, it hit me! What about my mantra to "be who I is"? I realized that not only did I not like being "Ms Tough," I was never going to be her. "Ms. Tough" was not who I was. I am someone who has a passion for bringing out the best in others and learning to flex my approach to individual styles. This passion is my talent.

My quest to be "Ms. Tough" ended when I decided to stop fighting my natural tendencies (my talent) and began implementing the mantra I swore to uphold back in high school. Changing me was no longer the focus. Instead, I started working on finding how to make "who I is," work for me. That's when I started leveraging my talent.

DISCOVERING WHO YOU ARE

Research has proven that when you do what you are both good at and enjoy, you are not only more successful, you are much happier with your life. Most of us can enjoy our jobs more when we can be who we are. If you are happier, you do a better job and everyone wins.

So who are you? What are your talents, strengths and attributes? Many women tell me that they have a difficult time answering questions about their abilities. They seldom take the time to think about what positive attributes they are bringing to the table. However, if you were to ask them about a co-worker, a friend or their children, they could rattle off a long list.

On the other hand, most of us can rattle off with ease our many weaknesses. If you don't know your talents, you are missing a great opportunity to leverage your unique attributes. All of us come with unique attributes that can help us reach our goals. However, we must know what they are before we can strengthen them and make them work for us.

There are many ways to help you identify your talents and strengths. Many assessment tools are available online, in books or you can find many consultants who are certified to assess talents and strengths.

A quick and dirty way to determine your natural talents is to think of the things you enjoy the most or what comes easily for you. For instance, do you have a knack for diffusing intense situations, solving complex problems, making people laugh, paying attention to details, selling ideas, etc.? Chances are the things you do well or enjoy are your talents.

In order for talent to flourish and companies to grow, they must select the right talent while ensuring it fits the organization, team and position. However, investing in the development of talent in an organization is a critical ingredient for growth. Talent Plus captures this idea in their Growth Formula:

(Talent + Fit) x Investment = Growth - Trademark of Talent Plus

(First, you select the right talent and ensure fit. Invest in talent through development, recognition, mentoring, coaching etc. If you do that, you will see growth in market share, revenue, productivity, service, etc.)

The popular book, *Strengths Finder 2.0*, by Tom Rath, offers an off-the-shelf assessment tool (that comes with the purchase of the book) and is designed to help you identify and rank your strengths based on 34 themes. This is a great tool because not only does it help you discover your strengths, but it also provides you with an action-planning guide to apply them as well.

According to *Strength Finders,* a talent becomes a strength once it is developed. In other words, one may have several talents. However, if they are never developed, they will not be strengths. This theory goes hand-in-hand to what Talent Plus describes as "investing" in talent.

A few years ago, I took the *Strengths Finder 2.0* assessment and the following are my top five strengths:

1. *Futuristic*
2. *Learner*
3. *Positivity*
4. *Ideation*
5. *Individualization*

I found this assessment to be right on. Embracing these strengths, I leverage them every day in my business, in my relationships as well as in helping others. Once you indentify your talents, develop them into strengths and then you can make them work for you.

MAKING YOUR TALENTS WORK FOR YOU

Successful people know their talents and leverage them to achieve their goals. Your talents are your competitive advantage over others in the marketplace. It is something that no one can take from you. When you leave an employer, your talents go with you. Your talent is also something you can grow and strengthen. Therefore, the more you use it, the stronger it gets, thus increasing your marketability.

LEARNING HOW TO ENHANCE AND LEVERAGE YOUR NATURAL TALENTS

Renowned leadership expert, John C. Maxwell's book, *Talent is Never Enough,* cites 13 key choices that you can make to become 'a talent-plus' person. They are as follows:

1. *Belief lifts your talent*
2. *Passion energizes your talent*
3. *Initiative activates your talent*
4. *Focus directs your talent*
5. *Preparation positions your talent*
6. *Practice sharpens your talent*
7. *Perseverance sustains your talent*
8. *Courage tests your talent*
9. *Teach-ability expands your talent*
10. *Character protects your talent*
11. *Relationships influence your talent*
12. *Responsibility strengthens your talent*
13. *Teamwork multiplies your talent*

There are various ways you may enhance your talents such as:

- ◎ Seeking mentors or a coach
- ◎ Obtaining career counseling
- ◎ Reading the latest books, articles and journals of your profession
- ◎ Reviewing online training materials
- ◎ Studying audio and video training programs
- ◎ Taking personal development courses and seminars

STRENGTHENING YOUR TALENTS

You can strengthen your talents by taking different levels of responsibilities at work. Often I advise my clients to consider lateral moves over promotions within their companies. A lateral move is a way to diversify your job experiences, while increasing your actual knowledge and skills. A focus on developing cross-functional skills will enhance your talents and help turn them into strengths. Many of us still have our eye on climbing the ladder as a way to get ahead. Therefore, we often miss other great opportunities to learn and grow.

Don't underestimate the advantage of having cross-functional experiences. They will give you an opportunity to work all of your talents. It is like working out using all of your muscles and consequently increasing your overall strength. Instead, many of us just work on a few muscles, thus only building strength in isolated areas.

WHY YOU CAN'T IGNORE YOUR WEAKNESSES

Although it is important to identify your talents, you should also know *your* weaknesses. However, *knowing* your weaknesses and *working* on your weaknesses are two different things. Let me explain:

Knowing your weaknesses is important because to be successful, you must learn how to get around them. For example, if *"attention to detail"* is not your strength, and details are important to your job, you must determine how you will be effective without that strength.

To be successful, you could consider the following options:

- ◎   *Delegating the details*
- ◎   *Teaming with another whom has that strength*
- ◎   *Establishing a foolproof system of checks and balances to ensure you don't miss details*

Knowing your weakness is also important in selecting jobs, teams and bosses. If you are more of an independent worker and the culture of a potential team requires collaboration, you may want to consider how you will get around that.

Although strengthening your talents is where you get the biggest bang for your buck, knowing your weaknesses is critical.

Working on your weaknesses is where most of us spend our energy. We spend dollars, time and energy trying to fix what we see is broken. We often become frustrated when we don't see progress. This lack of progress chips away at our confidence and further perpetuates our feelings of inadequacy.

Often we believe that we have to be masters of all areas. Many of us strive to be well-rounded leaders, proficient in all competencies. However, this belief leads us down the path of expending energy where we get a small return. Successful leaders enhance their natural talents and find other ways to complement their weaknesses. When I hear a women say that she needs to work on being something that I know she will struggle to become, I don't bite my tongue. Instead, I tell her to use her time more effectively by enhancing where she is already strong.

Extra Toppings to Enhance Your Sandwich

- ◎ Playing to your talents
- ◎ Developing your talents until they become strengths
- ◎ Matching job or careers to make the best of talents
- ◎ Selecting organizational cultures that reward your talents

Sure-fire Ingredient #3
A Golden Reputation

"When it comes to getting a job, rarely are you selected solely on how smart you are. You are most likely selected based on the feeling or expectation people have about you. This expectation is based on your reputation." --Jocelyn

EXECUTIVE CHEF

Robert Riney | President and Chief Operating Officer Henry Ford Health System

A Heart to Heart Discussion on a Golden Reputation with Robert Riney, President & COO, Henry Ford Health System

"My reputation has been more responsible for my career journey than anything else. Trust and reliability is what people gravitate towards. If you can make that effortless, people will respond positively to you. I have been very purposeful about my reputation."
--Bob Riney

I originally met Bob Riney when I came to interview for a position at Henry Ford Health System (HFHS) in 2003. Bob interviewed me for a position as a senior consultant for diversity. His unconventional approach immediately put me at ease. This comfort was a great support since interviewing with the senior vice president of human resources (the position he held at that time), who also stood a towering height of 6' 4" was a bit intimidating.

After inviting me to sit down, Bob said, "I am sure you have been asked many typical questions already as part of this interview process. Therefore, I will not be redundant.

To get this far in the selection, you must be qualified. So I am not interested in your qualifications. What I am interested in is what makes you tick."

Before I knew it, I was telling Bob about my passion around people and diversity. We talked about my values and the influences my mother had on me. Having the opportunity to discuss my interests both professionally and personally left me wanting desperately to become a part of the Henry Ford family.

I was ecstatic when I got the job. However, the best part was that I gained a mentor in Bob. He has provided me with short tidbits of wisdom throughout my tenure at HFHS and has taken an interest in my development. He has

*also served as a supporter, role model and most
importantly showed me the importance of a
solid reputation.*

BOB'S CAREER JOURNEY

*"I am the unique poster child of internal develop-
ment."* Bob Riney describes his journey as unique and
different from what he ever pictured. He arrived at HFHS
by *"accident."* Originally interested in criminal law, his
early career started at the Wayne County Youth Home in
Detroit. One of his responsibilities was to interview youth
with heinous crimes."

He found himself interviewing teens charged with
murder, and being young himself at the time, he found it
very disturbing.

*"The crimes were horrific, but once you stripped away
the veneer, they were just scared children,"* described
Bob.

This experience created an interest in him to help
improve society. He knew he wanted three things in his
career at that time: to be successful, to make money
and to improve society. Soon he found himself with a
job in health care at Henry Ford Health System. Being a
young professional, he found the job to be convenient
and a good place to make some money.

When he arrived at Henry Ford Health System, even
at an entry-level position, he was able to see that health
care was a big business. It was then that he realized
he got more than what he had bargained for. He also
learned that health care was complex. The complexity

was intriguing to him. He discovered his passion for caring for people and realized that health care was a great fit because of its important mission and its ability to improve the community.

According to Bob, there were three components that contributed to his early success: his interest in learning about the business; his willingness to ask questions; and most importantly, his recognition of individuals who were willing to take him under their wings and introduce him to others who helped him grow.

Bob's first professional job at HFHS was in human resources. He was hired as a recruiter, hiring for entry-level type jobs. As a recruiter, the best part of that job was that it also came with the responsibility of running new hire orientation. Taking new recruits on tours gave him access to meet people all over the company.

"In order to take people around the organization and give them a great experience, you have to really know the place. Therefore, I got to know the organization inside and out. " - Bob

Soon, he was meeting people all over the hospital. He had permission to spend countless hours with others and shadow them in their departments. This was a special part of the job he loved the most.

"Recruitment was like getting to know people and what makes them tick and whether they are going to

fit. I always saw the company as my own store, and recruitment as selecting the right people for my store."
-Bob

Bob later moved into employee relations, which allowed him to work in *"gray matter and complexity"* which he loved. He viewed employee relations as not having right or wrong answers, but shades of gray.

During his time in employee relations, he was living check-to-check. However, it was also at that time when he was given the most amazing professional career advice. The advice was to take a position as a compensation analyst. His first reaction was *"why?"* He had always liked working with people. Sitting behind a desk crunching numbers was not at all appealing. On top of that, it was a lateral move.

However, he took the advice and moved into an office the size of a closest, without a window. Being a guy of great stature, this was a tight squeeze. Day after day, he sat for hours crunching numbers. Although he knew this role was not going to suit him long-term, he found it beneficial as he learned a science and discipline that served him well later in his career.

Bob eventually went through all roles in human resources and finally landed a leadership role as corporate director of employee relations. By this time in his career, he had earned the reputation of *being reliable, having a lot of energy, being a creative problem-solver and delivering on promises*. This gained him the benefit of being a trusted advisor to senior leadership even though he was not the senior executive in HR (Chief Human Resources Officer, CHRO) at the time.

Due to his reputation, the CEO of the organization would frequently invite him to his office and ask for his advice and counsel when he was thinking of major organizational changes. Soon Bob was included in a small circle of trusted advisors. This developed into an *"amazing relationship with the CEO, which became widely known."*

Soon, Bob took another risky and unpopular move. He left his corporate position that gave him frequent access to the CEO and other influential leaders, to take a field HR leadership role at one of the community hospitals. Many of his colleagues told him he was crazy to make such a move. However, one person gave him great advice. He was told, *"The relationships you created in corporate are because you've earned them through your reputation. You have to have confidence that they are not going to go away unless you let them go away. Put that aside, and decide if the learning you will get with this new role will be important to your career."*

He took the job and gained valuable experience in which he would have never gained in the corporate function alone. Based on the advice he received, Bob found ways to stay connected and relevant with his corporate relationships.

Ultimately, Bob was promoted to Chief Human Resources Officer, (CHRO) of the System. He continued upward to Chief Operating Officer (COO), (a role that had been untouchable for someone who had never been a CEO of one of the hospitals). His reputation gave Henry Ford Health System's president & CEO confidence that he could do the job.

Many of the people who thought his career moves were crazy; have found that their careers have stalled as his propelled forward. He navigated his own career path strategically. However, he also acknowledges that he had great people who helped guide him along the way.

BOB'S PERSPECTIVES ON GOLDEN REPUTATIONS
(in his words)

When it comes to reputation, although it may sound trite, you have to start with a fundamental belief that you owe people authenticity. By that, I mean a what you see is what you get persona.

The best compliment I get is when I run into a housekeeper I hired 30 years ago, or a director of a department who knew me at various points of my career say that I have not changed. The truth is that I have changed a ton. However, what they are evaluating are my values. Those have not changed. This is the key to reputation. There is a distinction between values and behaviors. Therefore, my behaviors have changed, but my values, fundamental beliefs have not.

People will adapt to any style you bring to the table as long as they have some sense of predictability. People respond badly to not knowing who is going to show up; will it be the good leader or the evil twin. Be true to who you are and be comfortable in who you are.

There are three reputation pressures points that help you in your career:

1. **Reputation with your boss:** They have to see you as having their best interest at heart and that of the organization. You have to be 100% trustworthy and reliable. There is a tendency for people to vent about their bosses. This does not make you a bad person, but it does not instill trust. Things always come back. There are only two people I would vent to about my boss: my spouse and my coach.

2. **Reputation with those above and below you.** This comes from your relationships and reputation with stakeholders at all levels inside the organization and those in the community. I wanted employees at all levels running to my boss and telling them good things about me. This reputation with stakeholders influences the decision making for your career. This lets them (your boss) know what you are bringing to the table.

3. **Reputation within the community.** It is important to have my boss, while out at social events, have someone come up and compliment my work, efforts and behaviors. When there is a promotional opportunity, you want your superiors or the decision makers to have unsolicited information about you.

Your reputation is not a soft thing; it's a strategy. You have to have a strategy to position yourself for advancement. You can have multiple goals for behaviors. Therefore, you can make moves that can help your community that is selfless, while being strategic to help your reputation that is selfish. People get confused because they think in order to be selfless and selfish, it has to be mutually exclusive.

I watched some tragedies unfold with some people's careers relative to their reputations. When I see that, I make it an obligation to point it out to them. What I see most often, is what I call the "Macaroni and Cheese Behavior"- because it feels good, but if you do too much of it, it comes back to bite you. This is what happens when people go out with their colleagues and vent. It feels good but like macaroni and cheese, it always comes back. It is a short-term feel good. There is a naiveté that people don't believe what they say will come back to bite them.

The second thing I see is that people are now taking their venting from the bar to the social media. I never settle things or conflicts via email. They create a permanent record of what you say. It is a great way to get a bad reputation.

Another thing I have seen is crossing the line between having a healthy ego and becoming a narcissist. Some people get so addicted to needing to be validated and praised, that if they don't get it, they start manipulating things to get it. It is like an addiction. Unintentionally, they set up this aura that they need continuous praise that falls into the saying, "Don't bring me no bad news."

Stellar leaders have had their reputation destroyed because things were falling apart around them and no one let them know because they had sent up a message that "I want praise not negativity." It is a powerful thing that has destroyed careers. Therefore, I tell my team to tell me the good, bad and the ugly.

The downside to having a good reputation is that you get used to hearing people tell you how good you are. After awhile, you begin to believe your own press. You can become blinded to your weak points and soon forget that they exist. You can get into big trouble when this happens.

You have to have a long-term view when it comes to reputations. It is not about building a big peak and there you are standing on top of the mountain. Because, where do you go from there?

Reputations can become tarnished. Once I knew of a leader who was extremely talented with good results, but had a reputation of being a bully and being downright mean. Because they were getting great results, they felt that would seal their success. Besides their bullying reputation, they had also been going around attempting to tarnish other senior leaders' reputations. They were saying negative things about leaders, attacking them both professionally and personally.

Based on their reputation, they could have been fired. Instead we decided to confront the individual and bluntly asked for their re-commitment. After getting a coach, apologizing to those whom they crapped on, this individual changed their behavior and actually rebuilt their reputation.

To rebuild a tarnished reputation, it requires 100% ownership. It helps to go public, stand up and apologize by admitting to wrongdoing. As you advance, it requires your reputation to be more consistent.

People often confuse reputation with appearance. To me, my reputation is about my values. I really don't care if someone sees me on the weekend in clothes that don't fit my role or if they see me dancing badly. Some people also think having a good reputation means "never letting others see you sweat." Therefore, even on weekends, they are always in their uniform. It is so liberating to get past that. It goes back to "what you see is what you get." People are going to only expect perfection if that is the image you are portraying. It is a self-fulfilling prophecy.

When it comes to men and women around reputation, I hesitate to generalize. However, the differences I see is that women probably have worried more than men about the total package in reference to their brand, instead of what they bring to the table from an intellectual standpoint. There is so much pressure on women to define themselves by their total package. That is changing, however. Today, you see women leaders coming in all different types of styles. This is growth.

Men have historically built their brands in forums that have occurred in informal but powerful settings. Women are often disadvantaged because often they are usually the ultimate caregivers and couldn't engage in these off-hours activities. Men took well advantage of that. This is changing as well. Women are creating their own circles of influence. For some, it is the traditional activities such as the golf clubs, but others are starting things like book clubs to build their brands. I suggest that you follow the path that works for you.

A CLUB SANDWICH STORY

A colleague of mine, whom I will call Betty, came storming into my office one Friday afternoon. She was visibly upset and close to tears. After asking her what the problem was, she immediately went into a small rage.

She proceeded to tell me that she was "sick and tired" of the discrimination that was occurring in the workplace and that she was fed up. Having been turned down "again" for a promotion had her at her wits end. Betty, an African American professional woman with a master's degree, several years experience and multiple certifications, felt she had outgrown her current position and she deserved a promotion.

On a quest to move into leadership, she had applied for several promotional opportunities over the last three years without much luck. Feeling more than qualified for the jobs in which she had applied, she felt only discrimination could explain her rejection. She was angry, frustrated and hurt. Confused by her lack of advancement, she was stumped on what was holding her back. She desperately asked for my opinion on what she should do next.

Although Betty was stumped on why her career was stagnant, I was not. The answer to why Betty was not moving up was clear to me. It all boiled down to her reputation.

Although it was not an easy discussion, I told Betty what she needed to know. She had to face the cold fact that her reputation was the barrier to her advancement and she needed to salvage it if at all possible. Although she was hurt at first, she accepted responsibility for its restoration, even though her tarnished reputation was not all her fault.

THE TRUTH ABOUT REPUTATIONS

When it comes to reputations, I can't tell you how many times I've witnessed someone's reputation save them from disaster. Your reputation is like your personal brand. It speaks for you when you are not there. It is what people think about you when they hear or see your name. It is what you leave behind when you meet someone, or finish a class or go to a job interview. Reputations can get you business deals, jobs, promotions and the right contacts.

Your reputation is built on what you say, how you look, what you do and what you don't do. Therefore, is it important to think about what people are saying and thinking about you. Then ask yourself what do you want them to say and think about you and make sure you are living up to it every day.

There are many smart people with poor reputations who can't get the time of day from others. Many of them have no idea why they don't get callbacks, jobs, promotions, or even the benefit of the doubt. Your reputation travels fast. If it is bad, it travels much faster.

When it comes to a reputation, it can take a lifetime to build a great one, but it can take only a second to tarnish it. At the end of the day, it may be all that you have. Keep it polished like gold and you will be able to cash it in.

Above is an excerpt from the "seven life lessons" the theme for a commencement speech I gave to the 2010 graduating class of Baker College of Allen Park, Michigan.

According to David F. D'Alessandro's in his book, *Career Warfare: 10 Rules for Building Your Successful Brand on The Business Battlefield,* "People are constantly taking the measure of your character in a career. You have to behave in a way that encourages them to trust you and believe in you every minute of every day."

D'Alessandro makes the point that,

"Even not so smart organizations have figured out that they cannot afford to hire and promote people of questionable repute. This means that the single most important thing you can do for your career is to lay the groundwork for an attractive personal reputation, so that the next time someone powerful does think of your name, that person thinks well of you."

Your reputation is what builds your career both in the present and in the future. You will have a difficult time moving anywhere within your organization if your reputation is poor. A great reputation is not only important to gaining credibility, but it also places you in the best of positions for future rewards within the company. A positive reputation should be at the core of your career.

"No matter what, whatever you accomplish on a job will be forgotten over time. No one will remember the great job you did. However, your reputation may live in their minds for a lifetime." -Unknown

When it comes to getting a job, rarely are you selected solely on how smart you are. You are most likely selected based on the feeling or expectation people have about you. This expectation is based on your reputation.

George Foreman, the author of *Knockout Entrepreneur* and multi-venture entrepreneur champ believes strongly in the power of a "knockout" reputation. Although George Foreman is known for being a former boxing champ, it is his *George Foreman Grill* (100 million units sold worldwide) that made him a household name.

George claims that it was his reputation of being a "winner" that allowed him to launch his incredible enterprise that is now worth hundreds of millions. According to Foreman, a reputation of trust and wins will get you the credibility needed to be successful. Foreman also stresses that trust is built on, "relationships, consistency, and deliverables."

Many of us don't have any idea of what our reputations are. I've heard many women described as being "a complainer, weak, incompetent, lazy, trouble-starter, standoffish, sleazy, slacker, liar, etc. and they never had a clue that was being said of them. And if they did, they underestimated its damaging effect, especially on their future.

Believe it or not, your boss is the keeper of your reputation in the past and in the future. Therefore, leaving a job with an intact relationship with your boss should be a priority. The damage to your reputation is even more profound if negative words come from your boss. So be sure to feed your boss with good experiences, thoughts and accomplishments.

Those, who understand the power of a boss, understand the importance of keeping a boss happy. Making your boss's job easier, refraining from causing them too much grief and being dependable are all ways to help your boss look good. Also, your boss must feel that he or she can trust you. Therefore, building a trusting relationship is critical. Never bad-mouth a boss. They will always find out and you can best believe that your reputation will be destroyed after that.

When it comes to your boss, it is also important to know whether your boss is boosting or busting your reputation. If you don't know, you better find out. If your boss is a booster, you are golden, for now. However, don't sit on your laurels. The situation can change at a drop of a hat. A good relationship must be maintained, cultivated and kept fresh.

If, on the other hand, your boss is a reputation buster, try to rebuild the relationship immediately. Periodic pulse checks on the status are critical. The best thing your boss can do for you is giving you a good reputation. No raise, good performance appraisal or promotion can pay off more than a good reputation. So, don't get your priorities mixed up. Focus on getting the best return on your hard work and getting paid with a golden reputation.

A TUNA-MELT SANDWICH STORY

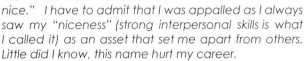

I grew up believing that names would never hurt you, until I entered the world of corporate America.

Years ago, I learned that I had been named "too nice." I have to admit that I was appalled as I always saw my "niceness" (strong interpersonal skills is what I called it) as an asset that set me apart from others. Little did I know, this name hurt my career.

Although I was "well- liked," "talented and smart," based on a "name," higher-ups were afraid to put me in situations where they thought I may get eaten alive. Therefore, I was not selected for specific promotional opportunities.

On a quest to understand my reputation, during a routine supervision meeting with my boss at the time, instead of the usually babble, I asked her frankly why I had hit a career roadblock and what did she think of me professionally. She told me straight; everyone liked me, but I was "too nice" for certain positions that may require me to be tough.

Just like that, I had the answer. All the time, I thought it was because I didn't have the right experience or credentials. I never thought it had to do with being called "too nice."

Interestingly, to my surprise, my name came from a single incident, when a "witch on wheels" (that was her reputation) challenged me during a presentation. I was so caught off-guard by her rude approach, that I allowed myself to get off-track. After the meeting, I forgave myself for the stumble and thought that my track record would protect me. That's where I went wrong. Instead, that one incident left me with a reputation that prevented me from moving forward.

Had I not asked my boss for feedback, I would have gone along blindly with a roadblock in my path.

Names are everything in the world of business. Decisions involving jobs, promotions, demotions, salaries, perks, etc. are made based on names. No matter how talented you are, the names determine how far you will go.

My story taught me that names stick to us like glue in the workplace and especially if you are a leader. Maybe it's because we are in the minority in leadership and with fewer numbers, our mistakes or mishaps are never forgotten. Our professional reputations are extremely fragile and we have to handle them with care.

So what names are people calling you? Are you called a people-person or a "B" on wheels, a friend or backstabber, a pushover or ultra powerful, innovative or stuck in your ways, frumpy or professional? If you don't know, you could be in for a rude awakening. Every women needs to know her "names" to get ahead in business. So, do you know yours?

My Tuna Melt story taught me valuable lessons about how much power reputations have in your career. The big lessons I learned are:

BIG LESSON #1: *REPUTATIONS ARE FRAGILE*

You can spend years building a strong reputation and it can be shattered by one incident. You and your actions are under constant scrutiny. People are making judgments about you with every encounter and forming new opinions every day. People talk and spread names throughout organizations. Therefore, you have to realize that it's "show time" every day and you must come with your "A" game.

Now, everyone makes mistakes. However, never let one go without putting forth effort to recover your reputation. If I had not been so self-absorbed after my mishap, I would have realized that I was being judged on how I handled the situation. I did not come prepared for the unexpected.

BIG LESSON #2: *BE OPEN TO FEEDBACK AND ACCEPT WHAT YOU HEAR*

It is not easy to hear negative things about yourself. But if you never hear the bad things, you can't fix them. So when you ask for feedback, stress that you want honest feedback. And then, take it like a woman. Although appalled, knowing "my name" empowered me to save my reputation. And that's what I did.

My boss did me a big favor. She gave me good, honest, feedback that helped propel me forward. If you don't feel comfortable approaching your boss, consider peers, mentors and friends as information sources. Sometimes your saboteurs can be a great wealth of information. Most will find joy in telling you what names you have.

BUILDING YOUR REPUTATION

When it comes to earning your reputation, determine what you want others to think about you, then set out to make their thoughts a reality. Evaluate how you are showing up to work. Are you showing up prepared, dressed appropriate for your role, and with the right attitude? It is important to dress according to the reputation you wish to earn. Remember the saying, "don't dress for the job you have, but for the one you want"? The same goes for your reputation. Therefore, if you want to be viewed as a competent leader, then don't dress like the opposite.

Once a client said to me, *"If I get that promotion, I am going to buy myself some executive –looking suits."* I stopped her immediately and told her not to wait until she got the promotion. I advised her to get the suits right away so she could begin building a reputation of being an executive, regardless of the promotion. You don't have to wait to build a reputation for what you aspire to be. You can start building it today.

Standing out from the crowd is another way to help your reputation. Therefore, find ways to convey what you are bringing to the table, what you want, and what differentiates you from the rest. You must let your employer (or customers for businesswomen) know why they should hire you, promote you or keep you.

When thinking about your reputation, keep in mind that people tend to do things for those whom they like. According to research by Harvard Business School's professor Teresa Amabile, people assess others through their warmth and their level of competence. That research also proved that being seen as tough or even mean, helps perpetuate the perception of competence. In other words, people who are viewed as tough or mean are believed to be more competent than those who are viewed as nice or soft.

In the paper titled, "Brilliant but Cruel," Professor Amabile's research revealed that although those who were viewed as nice were perceived to be warm, this niceness led to the perception of being weak and less intelligent. This idea goes against what most of us women are taught. We are socialized to be nice and not to hurt other's feelings. Thus, we are often viewed as weaker and less competent. This study made me think back to the reputation I had earned as "being too nice" in the past.

HOW TO PROTECT YOUR REPUTATION

Here's a short list of reputation destroyers. Avoiding these will go a long way to helping you to maintain yours:

Dating co-workers, revealing or inappropriate dress, gossiping, bad-mouthing a boss, drinking too much, weak handshake, poor hygiene, breaking promises, unreliability, tardiness, being unprepared.

The more successful you are, the more important your reputation becomes. Your reputation can open doors and your reputation can close doors. Therefore, be sure to maintain it for today for what you may want tomorrow.

HOW TO RESTORE A TARNISHED REPUTATION

Many women ask me how I restored my reputation after earning the name "too nice." Below are the steps I recommend if ever you find yourself in the position to restore you name:

STEP 1: Determine what reputation you want and design a plan to obtain it.

Once I discovered that my reputation was in need of repair, I took time to think through what reputation I really wanted. Knowing that I may only get one more chance, ensuring that I was building the right rep was important.

Therefore, my goal was to build a reputation as someone with great leadership, influence and strength. Once I had my goal established, I was ready to implement step 2.

STEP 2: Seek an opportunity to let you demonstrate the reputation you are seeking.

I searched long and hard for the right opportunity that would let me demonstrate my goal of leadership, influence and strength. Knowing that my boss was the keeper of my reputation (as all bosses are), I decided to target projects that would make her life easier and look great. In doing so, I knew I could stand a chance of restoring my reputation.

Then one day, the right project presented itself. My boss had a real problem on her hands. One of her departments had failed the quality assurance inspection for the third time and she had 90 days to turn it around. This department was known for major challenges like poor performance, many employee issues and complex problems.

I knew that if I could turn the department around, and demonstrate that I could handle the challenges,

I would be golden in the eyes of my boss. Therefore, I persuaded my boss into letting me take a stab at leading the area. Reluctantly she agreed.

In 90 days, the department went from the lowest quality scoring in the region, to the most improved. We passed inspection for the first time in three years. Of course, my boss was thrilled.

STEP 3: Promote your success loudly.

The last step I took was the most important. I made sure everyone in the company and my network knew about my success. Therefore, I asked my boss to endorse my application for the *"Presidents Award,"* a company-wide recognition for service excellence (which I won). I also submitted the new processes we put into place to the company's *"Best Practices"* newsletter. I even got our PR department to put my name in my college alumni newspaper as well.

Soon, I was known as the "turnaround leader" as coined by our regional vice president and was asked to join a task force team to help other areas with the same issues.

Those were the three steps that helped me restore my name and career. Now I make sure that I know the names I am called and if the wrong name appears, I know what to do.

Extra Toppings
to Enhance
Your Sandwich

- ◎ High quality work
- ◎ Consistency and predictable performance
- ◎ Reliability, dependability and kept promises
- ◎ Loyalty and trust
- ◎ Integrity

chapter seven

Sure-fire Ingredient #4
Effective Self-Promotion

*"I have always felt that there is nothing worse
than being successful and no one knows it. "*
–Jocelyn

EXECUTIVE CHEF

Jocelyn Giangrande
| President and Founder,
SASHE, LLC

**A "Keeping it Real" Discussion
About Self-Promotion**

*I*t took me years to understand the importance
of self-promotion. Being modest all my life,
promoting myself was uncomfortable. Even
when I forced myself to do it, I often felt guilty or
ashamed because I found it to be boasting or
self-serving. Therefore, much of my talent, ideas

and successes went unnoticed, untapped and unappreciated.

Most women shy away from self-promotion for the same reasons that I did. They see it as bragging, and distasteful. However, if done right, self-promotion is actually something that creates win-win situations for teams, organizations and customers. This is the true beauty of self-promotion.

It wasn't until I met a woman at a conference who was looking for "a good coach who specialized in professional reinventions," that I understood how self-promotion could help others. When I heard the woman's plea, I was able to conduct my first self-promotion in a way that made me feel like I was making a difference. I shared with her my experience and results in helping women reinvent themselves to revamp their careers. She was thrilled and together we found our win-win.

The funny thing about self-promotion is that it really isn't about telling the world how great you are just so that you can feel great. It is about telling what great things you bring that can help others solve problems, complete projects, produce results or bring people together. Learning how to let others know about your attributes and examples of what you have done successfully helps them see where you fit. Therefore, it is important to toot your horn to create these win-win situations.

Today, many people now call self-promotion "personal or professional branding." I believe women have adopted this term because it sounds less about "you" and more about your career. However, I see them differently. In terms of self-promotion, I see it as public relations. It's about positioning yourself well in the eyes of others. It is also about letting others know what your recent accomplishments are, what ideas you have and what special skills or qualities you bring. Letting others know what makes you special or differentiates you from the competition is critical in careers. Therefore, self-promotion is about keeping yourself front-of-mind when opportunities arise and keeping yourself fresh in the minds of others. In other words, self-promotion is like "selling yourself," without the hard sell.

Professional branding on the other hand, is more like your professional reputation. Your brand is what people think of you when they hear your name or see your photo. It is the reputation that you have built through your work, actions and attitude. Your brand is something that you build over time. Unlike self-promotion, your reputation (or brand) can be tarnished easily. Therefore, it takes constant polishing. Your brand is what people think you are. Self-promotion is what you tell them you are.

A REUBEN SANDWICH STORY

My education on the benefit of self-promotion came when a colleague of mine stopped me after a meeting. He told me that he wanted to help me grow my business and because he is well connected; he thought he could get me some business and help me make the right contacts.

He began by stating, "Lately, I have been going to many high-profile events with leaders whom you may want to meet. I often think about you, but I don't know enough about what you do, to make the introduction. You need to give me some sound bites so that I can help spread the word." He sounded frustrated.

It was then that I realized I was doing a poor job at self-promotion. Here was a person who was well connected and willing to toot for me. However, he didn't have the information to do the job properly. He also believed that I could help those in his networking circle. Helping those in his circle would be a win/win, thus the best type of connection.

That conversation helped me get my act together and start my own campaign to equip others with valuable information about my successes.

THE IMPORTANCE OF SELF-PROMOTION

Imagine if everyone you met were promoting the following about you:

1. What you do better than anyone else
2. What types of people, companies and businesses you have helped
3. Why you're passionate about what you do
4. How you can help others be successful

Now, imagine if no one was tooting anything like that about you.

Chances are, no one is promoting anything about what you do and how you have been successful in doing it. Most of the women I know, believe their bosses know how well they're doing. It wasn't until I became a leader myself, that I realized most managers don't have any idea about how well you're doing. Managers are too busy, too tired and too overwhelmed. Unless you place your accomplishments and successes right under their nose, they probably don't make the time or even have the time to notice.

This phenomenon is apparent during performance appraisal time. Most managers hate this time of year, because they haven't thought about your accomplishments in some time. This causes them to scramble, thinking about what to write about you and your performance. In most organizations a performance review is only required approximately once a year.

Consequently, most managers acknowledge your successes along with your weaknesses only during your annual evaluation. Therefore, if someone were to ask them how you are doing, depending on when they were asked, they may not have a clue. No one can toot for you if they don't have a clue about your current level of performance.

In this competitive job climate, you need everyone to be equipped with the most up to date information about your successes. That way, they will always have something to toot about!

WHY IT'S BETTER TO GET OTHERS TO TOOT YOUR HORN INSTEAD!

If you watch very successful leaders, you will notice that somehow their success stories always gets out. People tend to know what is going on with them professionally and personally. When they strike gold, everyone knows. Their accomplishments travel throughout organizations, networks and social circles.

Interestingly enough, most of the promotional information doesn't come from the leader directly. Instead, people willingly share it and spread the word for them. Now, don't get me wrong, the leader is very much responsible for getting the word out and many executives actually have their own PR team (that's how important self-promotion is). However, those who do it successfully, get the word out through others. They feed them information constantly in a package that makes it *easy* and *rewarding* to spread the news.

Spreading the news is very effective. According to principles pointed out in Malcolm Gladwell's acclaimed book, *The Tipping Point*, it is the second- and third-hand word of mouth that will create your biggest buzz. That is, your new clients are more likely to be people who heard about you second-hand rather than those who were in the audience for your presentations or who read your articles. When the information comes from a third party, it has more credibility. That is why testimonials are so effective.

The majority of successful leaders learn the importance of self-promotion early on and do it very strategically. They are very good at documenting their performance and they make sure that the *right* people in their network know about it.

THE SELF-PROMOTION PITFALL

Many of us see self-promotion as boasting, brown-nosing or simply a distasteful display of arrogance. Therefore, we avoid promoting our accomplishments at any cost for fear that others may think we are bragging. Consequently, we downplay our achievements. When it comes to promoting successes, women tend to give credit to everyone or everything other than themselves. We often say, "Well I have a great team." Or, "It was nothing," or "I couldn't have done it without so and so." On the other hand, men tend to take full credit for successes. They say, "Well what did you expect? You hired the best man for the job."

When it comes to failures, ironically, we take full responsibility. When a project falls short, we may say something like, " Well I tried." " I guess I didn't plan accordingly." And surprisingly, many of us will come straight out and say, " I take full responsibility." Men, however, often project the blame outward. They are more likely to say something like, "If we had better leadership on this project, we may have been able to execute more effectively."

Lisbeth McNabb, President of Women to Women Link, states that:

"In my 20s and 30s, I did not self-promote because I was so modest. I underplayed both my experience and strengths. Self-promotion can feel like not leveraging virtues. That is why personal branding is preferred as a word choice over self-promotion; we think good things about our brand because it's clear what the value statement is. It is not about being ego-driven. If people can learn how to make a statement about themselves in a way to find a win-win and find the person who needs or could benefit from what you have to offer, it can be a core business skill. Women are more modest than men and can really understate things. Men were especially good as mentors to help identify when I needed to say things better about myself. Listen and learn from those who are good about making self-promoting statements."

Bragging or boasting is frowned upon. I am sure you have come across a bragger in your past. They are painful to be around. No one wants to be viewed that way. Especially women. Therefore, we go to the other extreme. We spend our careers hoping that someone will take some interest in seeing how well we are doing. Often, we find ourselves feeling unappreciated, overlooked and taken for granted because no one is paying attention.

Many women believe that their hard work will get them to where they want to go. Therefore, many of us are working our butts off. Yet, we are not getting anywhere. Why? Many of us fall victim to the myth of hard work. Your hard work means nothing if no one knows how well you are doing, what your accomplishments are and how successful you have been.

I often tell my clients that there is nothing worse than being successful and no one knows about it.

Although we work hard, most of our superiors, networks and business contacts don't have a clue of how successful we are. We have not told them about our work. Your hard work will not pay off until you let people know what it is you are accomplishing.

If you are successful at your job, there are many ways to let others know. Here are three steps to help you do just that:

1. Take credit for your success.

Many of us also down play our accomplishments when someone pays us a compliment. Learning to say "thank you" sounds easy, but is difficult for most. When you have a success, learn how to take credit for it by saying "thank you." Try it for a week and let me know what you find.

2. Make yourself and your hard work known.

I bet you are accomplishing many things, but the world doesn't know. You don't have to scream from the rooftop, but you should come close to it. At a minimum, provide simple project updates that can be presented to your supervisor, department leaders or peers. This is a great way to let others know what you are accomplishing. If you just received a promotion, ask your PR department to write a release for you or at least put it in the company newsletter. Have a best practice;

ask to have a write-up in the company newsletter about your new process. This will get you recognition within your organization.

3. Ask for feedback.

If you are a bit modest, this may work for you. When you are working on an important project, ask for feedback from others in your network, from mentors or potential clients. This is an indirect way to let them know what you are doing and the complexity and level of expertise you have. People like to be asked for their input. However, by doing so, you are also letting them know more about your work.

Don't fall victim to the myth of hard work. Remember, it means nothing if no one knows about it. Get out and tell them what you are working with!

OTHER WAYS TO SELF-PROMOTION

There are many ways you may promote you without having to say a word. In fact, nonverbal communication helps send the message about what you bring to the table. Some ways you may promote yourself are as follows:

◎ Displaying certifications, diplomas and awards
◎ Wearing badges and lapel pins lets other know where you work, what associations you belong to or special certifications
◎ Maintaining an organized office, car and persona

- Displaying a positive and optimistic attitude
- Being prompt
- Delivering on promises
- Sharing business cards with information about your services, results and expertise
- Creating promotional profiles through social media and email signatures
- Using headers and footers on all presentations as self-promotional space. *Be sure to title all of your work.*
- Dressing professionally

Learning how to promote "you" without boasting or bragging is critical to career success. A good way to do it is to get others to do it for you. The important thing to remember is to not let your accomplishments go unnoticed. Shed the misconception or taboos about self-promotion, or you may find that you are a success, however, you are the only one who knows it.

Extra Toppings
to Enhance
Your Sandwich

- ◎ Learn to get others to toot for you
- ◎ Plan a promotional strategy and campaign
- ◎ Use your internal and external network to promote you
- ◎ Utilize the tools and vehicles around you to enhance your promotion
- ◎ Update your promotion as new accomplishments occur

chapter eight

Sure-fire Ingredient #5
Supportive Networks

"When it comes to networking, many of us still see it as selling ourselves to someone else, pretending to be interested in others, or asking for help when you need a job. Networking is none of that. Networking is about making connections with others, so that through your connection, you both benefit." -Jocelyn

EXECUTIVE CHEF

Lisbeth McNabb | CEO, W2W Link

An Open Discussion on Supportive Networks with Lisbeth McNabb, CEO, W2W Link

"Women tend to think of networking as asking others, (strangers) to do something for them. The majority of women don't think about it as a skill set. We tend not to think of it as a win-win. Instead we often view it as

going into a strange situation and handing out cards and pitching ourselves." -Lisbeth McNabb

Lisbeth was introduced to me through my network with Talent Plus. Once I heard of her background and most importantly that she and I shared the same passion, helping women advance their careers, I couldn't wait to connect with her.

Lisbeth is a warm and generous person who was eager to help me with this book project. In fact she responded within minutes of my invitation with a "How can I help?"

Discussing the importance of networking for women with Lisbeth was a wonderfully entertaining conversation of great stories, lessons learned and above all, a level of transparency that is not seen often. I felt like I was talking to an old friend who I could enjoy letting my hair down with and tell it like it is.

LISBETH'S CAREER JOURNEY

Lisbeth started building skills early in her career. She felt fortunate to have the opportunity to synthesize her passion with her strengths. When the two overlapped, her energy always increased. According to Lisbeth, when she didn't have passion for her work, her energy decreased. Through her moves across Telecom, the Airlines, consumer packaged goods, and online dating, innovation was the common thread.

She attended the University of Nebraska receiving a marketing degree. The then 22 year-old nabbed her first job with AT&T working in sales and marketing. This was during the post deregulation era. It was there that she realized that she had a passion for innovation and for doing things that hadn't been done before.

She established a pattern of five-year stints at companies that had high growth potential. She was never interested in going to the big stable parts of companies. Instead, she enjoyed areas that would allow her to leverage her strengths and passion, which happens to be discovering visions and results around business. She also has a passion to connect people.

Lisbeth has built on her experience as former strategist and CFO of match.com. Her professional history includes senior executive positions in finance and strategy at Pepsico, Frito-Lay and Sodexo Marriott.

Lisbeth has had many accomplishments and successes throughout her career. At Pepsico/Frito -Lay where she held an innovation leadership role, she led a high performing business unit team and took it from 20 million to 40 million. At Sodhexo she took her unit from half-billion to a billion. Even her time at Match.com as the chief financial officer helped take the company to high growth. According to Lisbeth,

> **"People thought I was hurting my personal brand by joining an online dating company."**

Lisbeth's professional memberships, activities and awards include: Women Corporate Directors; Finance

Executive International; Women Foodservice Forum; Texchange; Board Member of Nexstar; Nasdaq; Menttium and Southern Methodist University MBA Associate Board – mentoring program; advisor to a number of entrepreneurial companies, Design Block Zero, Noofangle Media and Women That Soar.

In 2007, she decided to start her own business, The *Women to Women Link* or w2wlink.com. *Women to Women Link* is the premier community dedicated to professional women, helping them get to where they're going – faster. The company provides expert knowledge and tools to overcome obstacles, and connect with others in the online groups. McNabb leads a team of professionals to research and meet the needs of the professional woman in content and networking aspects through targeted content and online marketing and proprietary software for online networking.

LISBETH'S PERSPECTIVE ON SUPPORTIVE NETWORKS *(in her words)*

> Networking did not come naturally for me. My networking skills had to grow over time.
>
> We have done a lot of research around networking and how people see it as a barrier. Women may have more people in their networks. However, men do tend to have stronger networks that stem from the beginning of their career. They tend to put "chips" in, with the plan to cash them in later; such as in business introduction, etc.
>
> Women will usually separate their social from their business relationships instead of thinking of leveraging those relationships as a win-win. When we see the power of what men do well and combine that with what we do well, which is having an expanded

network, we can integrate our relationships-- social with the business. Underestimating the value of "giving forward" is also a misconception.

We need to practice our sound bites for each other when we introduce one another. People are more interested when someone else introduces you. Networking along with skill building and leveraging your strengths is very important. Even if someone is going to have a 25- year career at one company, those who maximize their talents will still have to have networking skills, in order to excel in the company.

Networking has helped me in my love for innovation. Through networking, I was able to sell my vision for innovation and working it towards strategy and results. Through networking, I was able to get people in my network to know what I was passionate about. Many people say that I am the best "strategic connector," they know. I do have a servant leader attitude in me. I believe in abundance and giving forward to help others move forward. When it comes to networking, I believe I have some strengths and I use it to help others.

My six degrees of separation is really one-two degrees and is getting larger and larger as my career progresses. Therefore, keeping up with networking from a time perspective became a challenge. "I felt pained by my inability to meet people one-on-one." Therefore, I used my talent for innovation by setting aside time once per month to invite people to come together in a networking circle. This allowed me to support people and leverage my time more effectively.

If you really hate networking, I suggest you do it in pairs. However, be sure you pick the right person to represent you and to describe your brand. Like most of us, if we hate something, we feel a drain from it. Therefore, I suggest journaling about what you hate about it, what outcomes you want and what does successful networking look like to you. With that information, you can manage it accordingly. When you put something on paper, you can work through it.

Getting organized around your networking goal is also important. Most of us hate networking because we are not organized around it enough to feel effective. Getting organized makes it bearable.

Some networking rules I follow are:

1. Don't offer to introduce people to more then two-three contacts at a time. Most people can't follow up with more than that, including me. This protects my network and holds people accountable for reaching out to them.

2. Don't take cards if you don't plan to do anything with them. It is easy to accumulate a bunch of cards after an event, and then they lie there on your desk in a big pile. I only take cards I plan to use and I organize them accordingly. One process I use that has helped me be more efficient is to use the V-card* in my Outlook. When I am at an event, I pull up that V-card and ask if I may share my electronic card with them an hour later. That way it saves them extra work as well.

*The V-card is an electronic business card that has automated the traditional business card. It is a convenient way of exchanging personal information such as name, address, phone numbers and email addresses.

A TUNA SANDWICH STORY

Once I was hired to help a client (whom I will call Lisa) with her job searching strategy. By the time Lisa sought my help, she had been job searching for over 18 months. She was not unemployed, however, the job she had at the time, was something she described as "a keep the lights on" type of job and she absolutely hated it.

During our first session, she explained to me how she needed to get out of her current situation. Currently employed as a sales account manager, she found herself mix-matched with a job she took out of desperation. Lisa's background was in human resources (HR), a field where she had a successful career for over 13 years. Before being laid off, she had been a director and a member of her organization's executive team.

Having to take a non-leadership role in an area where she had neither experience nor passion, was wearing her down. On top of that, she also had a boss who she described as unprofessional, offensive and a micromanager.

Since taking the sales job, Lisa's income had taken a huge dive as well. Taking a pay cut was something that also had her concerned and ready to make a move. Her sales account manager job paid half of what she had made previously.

"I really need to get a another job," she stated with desperation. Even though she had been actively looking for over a year and had gone on many interviews, she had not landed a job. She was fed up and stressed.

"I don't know what I am doing wrong, but something is not working."

"I have tried everything." I have posted my resume on Career Builder, Monster and LinkedIn. I also review the job boards every weekend and apply to all the jobs in which I am qualified. I have even posted my resume with the Society of Human Resources Management (SHRM) as well. I have gotten some interviews, but I can't get a job. What else can I do?" she asked.

It was then that I asked her if she knew the number one way that people get jobs. She quickly answered, "Of course. The number one way is through who you know in your network."

She continued however by saying, "I know I should be networking, but I don't have the time for that. I need to find a job right now."

THE POWER OF NETWORKING

Lisa's story is not uncommon. So many women tell me that they don't have time to network although they know how important it is.

According to the Riley Guide's, *"The Art of Building Alliances,"*

"Obtaining a diverse network will expose you to individuals and groups of people with a host of different backgrounds, experiences and useful connections. Having a diverse network to draw from if used correctly can point you toward some very exciting and lucrative opportunities."

Tom Boyle of British Telecom coined the expression *NQ*, or *network quotient*. According to Boyle, a person's ability to form connections (that person's NQ) is more important to careers than their IQ.

Your network also determines your future as proven by Dr. David McClelland, a former professor of Psychology at Harvard University who studied human motivation. While researching the "qualities and characteristics of high achievers in our society," Dr. McClelland discovered that "successful people were systematically connected to other successful people." Therefore, he found that, *"we become like those whom we hang around."*

The people you hang with, what Dr. McClelland called your "reference group," is a major factor in determining your chances of success or failure. The more you hang with successful people, the more likely you are to be successful.

COMMON PITFALLS WOMEN FACE IN ATTEMPTING TO NETWORK

"I know I should be networking, but I don't have time" is what my clients repeatedly tell me.

The three most common complaints that I hear from women are:

- ◎ **Not enough time**
- ◎ **Don't know how to network**
- ◎ **Dislike of small talk**

Let's talk about these in more detail...

1. I don't have enough time

There is not a person on the planet that couldn't use more time. Time is one of the most precious things in our lives, especially for women. Unfortunately, we only get what we get. Therefore, prioritizing how we use our time is crucial.

When prioritizing your time, keep in mind that networking should be high on the list. Many of us cringe when we hear that. Because we are so busy, thinking of going to events after a long day is the last thing we feel like doing. I used to feel the same way until I found a networking loophole. The loophole is:

"You don't have to go to a formal event to network.
You can network anywhere, anytime, with anyone."
–Jocelyn

If you can learn to connect with people wherever you are and anywhere you find them, not only will you build your network, you will not have to add additional "networking time" to your already busy day. Once I learned to blend networking into my day, my actual networking circle tripled. The point is, you can learn to network anytime and anywhere. This is where understanding the difference between networking and connecting comes in handy.

My secret to getting around this barrier of time, was to learn to network "every day and everywhere. I started networking wherever I found myself. I networked in:

- Salons
- Grocery stores
- Sporting events
- Parent-teacher conferences
- Meetings
- Parties
- Airports
- Farmer's markets
- Concerts
- Weddings, etc.

Although I do believe in attending certain networking events, there are many other great places to network and many of us are missing great opportunities to connect with others by not taking advantage of these places. Because many of us have a narrow view of networking, we only think of formal networking events as the only place to make connections. However, there are

hundreds of places to network in that we frequent every day. Places like:
- The soccer game
- The mall
- The golf course
- The cleaners
- The doctor's office
- The art fair
- The fitness center
- The knitting/scrapbook class
- The veterinarian's office
- The post office

You could also network when you*****:
- *Attend professional or trade association meetings*
- *Volunteer for a local park "clean-up" day*
- *Visit with other members of your social clubs or religious groups*
- *Talk to your neighbors*
- *Strike up a conversation with someone else waiting at the dentist's office*
- *Post messages on mailing lists or in chat rooms*
- *Talk to sales persons who are visiting your office*

*The Riley Guide at www.RileyGuide.com

In order to be successful using this tactic, you must be sure to have business cards with you at all times. Whenever I leave the house, I always throw a couple of cards in my pocket. You must also be prepared with your 30-second introduction that we will discuss later in this chapter as well.

Connecting is the key to networking everywhere. We will also talk more about connecting later in this chapter.

2. I don't know how or where to network

The best advice I have about learning how to network is to **never** "network." That may sound odd. However, when people "network," they go into "sell mode" and that is not exciting for anyone. Instead of selling, focus on connecting with others. If you see networking as selling yourself to someone else, or pretending to be interested in others, or asking for help when you need a job, you miss the benefit of networking. Networking is none of that. The true networkers know that it works best when you connect with others for mutual benefit.

According to *RileyGuide.com*, a website that provides free career and employment information for job seekers, many people have misconceptions about networking.

Riley says:

"Networking isn't a process of making cold-calls to people you don't know. It's talking to people you do know or asking them to introduce you to others. Networking does not have to be a carefully choreographed process of meeting and greeting people. It's much better done on a more informal basis, but remember that networking is always a

two-way street. It must benefit both persons to be most effective, so as you ask your network for help when you need it, be prepared to return the favor when asked."

Networking is about making connections with others so that through your connection, you both benefit. The best connections I have made came from helping others meet their goals. If you can help others be successful, you will find yourself with a strong network (of highly satisfied people) faster than just looking out for your own self-interest.

Finding common ground is a quick way to build a connection. When I meet someone new, I try to find out more about him or her until I find our common ground. Once we discover what we have in common, I know we have made a connection that can be built upon. I keep track of our common ground and try to look for ways I can use it to help them reach their goals, whether professionally or personally.

One of the best professional connections I ever made came from helping someone personally. Once at a retirement party, I met a successful realtor. After talking for a moment, we both discovered that we had teenage sons who loved the same video game. She told me that her son had lost his game and was disappointed because now the game was very hard to find. She was hoping to surprise her son with another copy for Christmas.

When I got home, I informed my son about her dilemma. Surprisingly, less than a month later, my son found that rare video game at a rummage sale for $20. He bought it and gave it to me (I had to pay him back of course). You can imagine her pleasant surprise when she received it. That was the best $20 I ever spent. Because ot that connection, I received several client referrals and earned a lifetime friend. Although our connection was built on something that had nothing to do with business, it has turned into a mutual caring relationship with each of us looking out for the other, and providing each other with some great business connection as well.

Deborah Williams, senior vice president of human resources at Parkview Health in Indiana says it best. Her perspective on making connections is: "Every day we are talking to people at work, in the store at our place of worship. Everyone who knows me knows that I don't have any shame when it comes to making connections. Recently I have been having work done on my house and as a result, I have had all types of workers coming through my home. Somehow I find myself asking them "What does your spouse do?" Next thing I know we are exchanging business cards."

I have found and recruited several employees from this type of exchange. Taking the time to listen or engage in conversation may open doors that you may not have ever thought of.

3. Dislike of small talk

In my opinion, nothing about networking has to do with small talk. When I am making connections, I have sincere, meaningful conversations with people whom I sincerely wish to know better. Small talk is for the birds and not only a waste of valuable time, but a big turn-off as well. If you are sincere, you can always find valuable things to talk about. So if it is not genuine, why bother. Most people can see right through small talk anyway. When you talk without genuine interest in the other person, that is truly small talk.

Many women tell me that they are at a loss at knowing what to say, or how to start the conversation. Therefore, I suggest you prepare your 30-second introduction (we will discuss how to craft one later on in this chapter). Having a prepared introduction will boost your confidence and you will always know what you're going to say which can prevent you from fumbling when you meet others.

The next suggested tip is to make sure that you are up on current events. In the old days of newspapers, my mentors used to tell me to read one paper a day to stay current. Now however, social media tools such as Twitter, has made it easy to know what is going on in the world. By simply following news publications such as, *USA Today*, *The Wall Street Journal*, *Harvard Business Review* or *Newsweek*, you can greet others with up-to-date information. Following such publications will give you up-to-the–minute snippets to help you stay informed.

It is also suggested that you follow at least one sports publication. Although I am far from a sports enthusiast, I stay current in the area. There is nothing worse than finding out that the sports team in the city where you are networking, has just entered the playoffs, and you didn't have a clue. (That actually happened to me once. I was never more embarrassed). At a reception, a woman greeted me by saying, "Aren't you excited?"

"About what?" I asked. I had no idea that sports' history had just been made in that city that very day. She was baffled by my ignorance of the fact.

WHO SHOULD BE IN YOUR NETWORK?

Who to include in your network circle is another common concern. There are many effective methods you can use to increase your networking portfolio. Have you considered networking with past professors, fellow students or alumni? Also consider taking advantage of the various mixers and other social networking events that are offered every day in our communities. These events are not only fun, they are opportunities to meet new and exciting people. I often look in the social scene section of the local magazines and papers, in order to see who is mixing with whom and how I may fit in.

WOMEN AND NETWORKING

When it comes to networking, many of us still see it as selling ourselves to someone else, pretending to be interested in others, or asking for help when you need a job. Networking is none of that. Networking is about making connections with others, so that through your connection, you both benefit. Networking is an important ingredient to our overall strategy. It allows us to make the strategic connections we need to make in the world of business.

There is indeed a difference between how men and women form and use professional relationships at work. When it comes to size and the cohesiveness of their professional networks, research shows that women tend to be more effective at networking overall than men. However, it still does not compare to the concentration of power in male networks.

According to William Bielby, professor emeritus of Sociology and a leading researcher in race and gender bias at the University of Illinois at Chicago:

"Women have tended to be better connected overall, but they and many of their female contacts tend to work in more female-dominated jobs. So their networks may be wider but not reach to as high a level as men's, who tend to be better connected, particularly in getting professional news, to more high-status people."

Another interesting point is that although women network more than men, men tend to be more strategic in their approach. In general, men tend to build networks with those who will help them reach their professional goals. Whereas women tend to network with those who do the same types of work as themselves and also those with whom they enjoy socializing.

Networks are most productive when built on shared interests such as people you meet when you are working on a project or at a soccer game etc., not necessarily by formal professional networks. When it comes to job searching, I found that it was these informal relationships that I happen to build that were beneficial in getting me interviews. My formal corporate network was not helpful in finding a job because all of them had jobs and didn't know of other opportunities. Therefore, you never know what can cascade from such casual encounters. So be sure to capitalize on these relationships.

TOP NETWORKING PITFALLS TO AVOID

Besides mistaking networking for selling yourself, there are a few other networking pitfalls that often get in the way of career advancement. They are as follows:

1. Networking with the same circle of people.
Once we get a good circle of contacts, we tend to stay within that network making it our comfort zone. This is the number one mistake I see. Although it is easier to interact with those whom we know, it seriously limits your ability to gain new information, job leads and business contacts. To get access to opportunities and influential contacts, you must get out of your comfort zone and broaden your network.

Another good reason to broaden your network is that studies have shown that the people who are the most successful in finding new jobs, additional business contacts and important information actually found their leads from networking with people whom they barely knew. In other words, when we network with those whom we know well, we are less likely to get new information.

Those whom we know usually have the same access to information that we have, thus we are missing out on the vast pool of information and leads that are generated outside our circle. To prevent this, be sure to diversify your networks and broaden your circle.

A great example of the benefits of a broad network is that of heroes of the American Revolution—Paul Revere and William Dodge. The reason why everyone remembers Paul Revere and not William Dodge—although both were messengers of the Revolution—is that Paul Revere had a diverse network that came from natural relationships and shared interest. William Dodge, on the other hand, did not have a diverse network. Instead it was made up of like-minded individuals who did the same professional work as him. Even though William Dodge actually talked to more people the night the British were coming, his network was less productive in spreading the word.

2. Networking only when you need a job.

I am sure you have heard of the cliché, "the best time to network is when you don't have to." This cliché is very true. Don't wait until you are desperate to start networking. Desperation is a turn off and will send most people running away from you. There is nothing more annoying than receiving emails from people you haven't heard from in years or worse, people you don't know, wanting to network because they need a job. When I receive such a connection request, (which I receive quite often) I ignore it as it goes against the whole concept of connecting. Networking is not just about you. Networking is about a mutual benefit. To me, it seems selfish to only think of your network when you need something.

Also, keep in mind that to build a good network takes time. Trying to do that when you are in desperate need of a job is difficult. Network when you don't need to. Then when you need help, your network will be there to offer assistance.

3. Failing to follow up with your network.

How many times have you heard, "let's do lunch sometime"? I have heard that a hundred times, however, only a handful of people actually contact me for lunch. Most, I never see or hear from until our next chance encounter.

If you connect with someone, be sure to follow up. My rule is to send an email within 24 hours of meeting someone. Comment on something you discussed and reconfirm the lunch if applicable. Then periodically send them a note, article or quote to keep the connection fresh.   I keep track of everyone in my network. I know where all my connections come from, and where they work and live. Then when I travel, I look them up and ask to reconnect. That is a great way to build a relationship and keep the connection fresh.

A dear friend of mine, Deborah Williams, senior vice president of human resources at Parkview Health in Fort Wayne, Indiana shared with me her opinions on networking mistakes. Deborah states:

"The time to build the networking relationships is before you need them. We all know of people we have not heard of since the last blue moon. Then they call you when they need a job, or need you to provide a reference for them and then you feel used. No one wants to feel used. Therefore, the best time to network is every day. Be open to helping other people. I like to put people in contact with one another who have common interests or who could benefit from knowing each other. Be open to building relationships. Sometimes it is as simple as putting people in connection with someone else."

PLANNING YOUR NETWORKING STRATEGY

As they say, *failing to plan is like planning to fail.* Unfortunately, many of us are planning the latter. Without a plan, many of us go out to networking events, and think that by chance, we will build a strong network. Most of us have a broad goal of networking. Usually the goal is to find people that will help us get a job, find new business contacts or obtain a mentor. However, because we have not planned beyond that, although we have gone to many events, we find ourselves without the network we need.

Failing to plan is the major reason why we don't obtain that effective network that will support our career or business goals. Many of us go out networking without a plan. This lack of planning leads to a waste of valuable time and frustration. Eventually we give up because we don't see a return on our investment.

When I work with clients, I share three basic steps I use to plan my networking strategy. The recommended steps are:

STEP 1: ESTABLISH YOUR NETWORKING GOAL

Whether you are networking to find a mentor, job, or for business contacts, every good strategy starts with establishing a goal. Ask yourself the following questions:

1. I am networking to accomplish… (What)?
2. I will network with… (Whom)
   to accomplish my goal?
3. I will network…(Where) to find them?
4. I will know I am successful (When)…?

STEP 2: DEVELOP YOUR 30-SECOND INTRODUCTION

Writing and practicing how you will introduce yourself in different settings will help with your confidence when initiating conversations. Adapting your introduction to different settings is important. You don't want to use the same intro for a professional/business setting as the one you would use at your neighbor's barbeque. When it comes to networking, your introduction is critical. More often than not, you may only have 30 seconds to intrigue a person enough to want to connect with you. Therefore, it is important to have a prepared introduction or brief commercial that you can use to spark interest.

Although, it takes some work, many of us fail to make connections with the right people because we don't sell ourselves quick enough. I suggest that everyone have a prepared 30-second commercial. It is important to have a prepared 'self promotional' commercial and be ready to market yourself on the spot. (Remember the Super Ingredients in Chapter 2, preparation, luck and opportunity?)

Every self- promotional commercial should answer:

1. Who are you and what do you do? (Be specific)
2. Who do you serve?
3. What benefits do you deliver or what problems do you solve?
4. What qualifications and successes do you have?

The self-promotional pitch I often use for professional networking settings goes something like this:

"Hello, I am Jocelyn Giangrande. I am a professional coach (who I am), however, the majority of what I do (what I do) is help women (who I serve) see where their careers may be taking a wrong turn (what problems I solve), or assisting women in making career transitions (benefits I deliver). Over the last ten years as a career strategist (qualifications), I've assisted hundreds of women in putting together career strategies that put them on the right track (successes)."

It is important to not sound like a robot when you are introducing yourself. I often take my introduction and try to put it in a conversational tone. I never say the above pitch verbatim. When someone asks me what I do, I may say something like this, which is a variation of my commercial:

"You know how sometimes you may find that your career is just not going where you want it to go or you are considering a transition all together? Well, over the last ten years, I have been working with women to help them find out why their careers are stagnant and how to turn them around. Often I help them to plan a strategy to get them where they want to go."

Again, you want to craft a commercial that peaks interest in the person so that you can build a connection.

STEP 3: PRACTICE

Practice your introduction in various settings and tweak it until you get it just right. Also, practice how you will answer certain questions. For example, a friend of mine avoided "networking events" because she was afraid that someone would ask her about what she did for a living. Being recently laid-off, she didn't know what to say. I advised her to prepare an answer that she was comfortable with beforehand, and use it when the subject came up. Armed with a prepared response, she started networking with more confidence.

The same was true with a contact of mine who had recently gone through a high-profile divorce. She avoided networking events because she didn't want to face the many questions people had regarding her situation. Once we worked through how she should respond, she was able to show her face again.

THE TRUTH ABOUT SOCIAL NETWORKING

Due to social networking and technology, instead of six degrees of separation, everyone you wish to connect with is now only four degrees or less. Once I read that, I looked at social networking from a new perspective. Instead of avoiding it, I embraced it as an effective tool.

Depending on your generation, you may have mixed views about the importance and value of social networking. So many women tell me that they don't know how to use social networking to get what they need. They are baffled because they have placed their profiles on sites, but "nothing is happening" they say. I used to say the same thing until I realized the secret to this type of networking.

The secret to social networking is understanding the "social" part of the term. You must participate or "socialize" to make it work for you. Let me put it this way, if you went to a networking event and didn't talk to anyone, would you be surprised when you didn't obtain effective connections? The same is true with social networking. You cannot just post a profile and expect to gain effective connections. You have to "socialize," get involved and participate to get the most out of it.

Social networking has really changed the networking arena, and has taken networking to a whole new art form. Today, the world can be part of our network in a stroke of the keyboard or a click of a button. We have the ability to keep our network up to date, up to the latest second. We have the ability to share with others what is happening with our careers, our personal lives and our thoughts. (There are parameters regarding what we should share.) We can even connect with authors, celebrities and successful CEOs.

There are many platforms available to keep us connected. My top three social networking tools are: *LinkedIn, Facebook and Twitter.*

LINKEDIN

LinkedIn is the number one professional networking site with over 90 million users representing 200 industries. It is hard to believe that it has only been around since 2002. However, it has changed the professional networking arena. According to LinkedIn, *"More than half of LinkedIn members are located outside of the United States. There were nearly two billion people searches on LinkedIn in 2010."*

There are many benefits to using LinkedIn. According to Shama Hyder Kabani, in her book, *The Zen of Social Media Marketing:*

"Currently, LinkedIn is great for staying in touch with other professionals and has been instrumental for many people in finding new jobs or business leads. It is becoming the number one source for

recruiters to find new job applicants and for businesses to find new contacts."

FACEBOOK

Facebook to some extent is great for staying connected to our friends, family and to exchange news about our lives and to share photos with one another. But, Facebook has the greatest potential to be used to network with a host of other professionals from a host of fields. Actually Facebook reaches a wider audience than LinkedIn.

Facebook, has 250 million active users compared to about 44 million for LinkedIn—even though the atmosphere is clearly not as focused on business, there are still a ton of opportunities for professional networking that business users would be remiss to pass up. Once you look beyond the obvious social features like sharing pictures and poking friends, there are plenty of ways to tap into the professional community on the world's largest social network.

Mashable, The Social Media Guide, written by Boris Epstein, CEO and founder of BINC; *How to: Use Facebook for Professional Networking* has a great list of social networking techniques for Facebook. They are as follows:

– If you have friends whose professional advancements you respect, go to their profile page and click on their info tab. Towards the bottom of the page, you'll see links to all of the groups to which they belong.

– On the main page of any Facebook Group, there are links to several other similar or related groups.

– Conduct an Internet search for "popular Facebook Groups" coupled with some of the keywords that interest you. You'll often uncover blog posts, articles and people tweeting about a variety of groups, some of which may interest you.

"Once you find a group that interests you, it's a good idea to evaluate whether or not it will be a good fit before joining and pouring too much time into it."

TWITTER

Twitter is part blog, part social networking and part instant messaging. It is a platform that gives the writer or "tweeter" 140 characters to answer the question "What are you doing?" People answer the question by "tweeting." People may become followers of your tweets and you may follow their tweets also if you wish. Believe it or not, Twitter is the fastest growing social networking site for 35-44 year olds. I find that people either love or hate Twitter. I have to admit, it had to grow on me as I hated it at first. Initially I didn't have any interest in knowing what people were doing all day long.

According to Twitter, in 2011, they had nearly 200 million Twitter accounts. However, not all accounts are active, meaning that those whom have accounts are not using them consistently. Most people use Twitter to follow individuals they have some interests in, such as celebrities, athletes and friends. Twitter has also been instrumental in emergencies to raise funds, find people and share information. If you need to spread the word, Twitter may be your best friend.

When I began to use Twitter, I realized that the key to using it effectively is not in answering the question "What are you doing?" literally. Instead it is best to answer *"What are you doing that is helpful to someone else?"* Realizing that, changed how I use Twitter and my overall satisfaction with the tool. Now, my tweets are designed to provide a snippet of useful information to my followers and engage them in dialog, inspiration and education. Twitter also allows you the ability to send direct messages, send links and most importantly, include searchable information by placing a hash symbol "#" in front of key words. This is useful when you are tweeting at conferences and want other attendees to find your relevant tweets. Doing so allowed my messages to be discovered by others who had my similar interests.

Another useful feature of Twitter is the ability to retweet (RT) someone else's tweets. This comes in handy when you come across something interesting that may be helpful to your community or your network. You may retweet it and get the information to your connections. We all know how important networking is, we just don't make the time to do it well. Having a diverse network of people in our professional and personal circles has the ability to expose us to others with a host of different backgrounds, experiences and connections. These connections can really enhance our knowledge base, our career goals and provide us with the chance to give to one another.

A good network can determine your future. The people you know and hang around determine your chances of success or failure. Learn to connect with people wherever you are and find your common ground. Remember that your Network Quota (NQ) is more important than your IQ. Connect every day everywhere.

Networking is a two-way street where each person obtains something from the process. Successful networks are always a win-win for all.

Extra Toppings
to Enhance
Your Sandwich

- ◎ Give first, before seeking to receive
- ◎ Find common ground
- ◎ Diversify your network
- ◎ Practice your 30-second introduction
- ◎ Connect every day and everywhere

Sure-fire Ingredient #6 Diverse Mentors & Sponsors

"Going the course is a challenging ride. Mentors with different perspectives, can help push you to grow and save you from disaster." -Jocelyn

EXECUTIVE CHEF

Jocelyn Giangrande |
President & Founder,
SASHE, LLC

A Frank Discussion on Diverse Mentors and Sponsors

I have never known a successful woman who did not attribute some, if not all, of her success to a good mentor or two. For women, mentors are the key ingredients to avoiding the land mines, pit falls and political blunders that are all over the place at work. Mentors are also credited with helping women

chapter 9

obtain the recognition, respect and effective communication skills critically needed for sustained career success. Although mentors play a significant role in long-term

careers, more women than not, report never having had one.

In his book, Never Eat Alone: And Other Secrets to Success, One Relationship at A Time, Keith Ferrazi, states,

"No process in history has done more to facilitate the exchange of information, skills, wisdom and contacts than mentoring."

In selecting a job, access to mentors is more valuable than any amount of compensation. We women are mainly socialized to work independently. We are taught from an early age to be responsible for our own success. We believe that if we work hard, we will be rewarded. We don't usually view success that is gained through the support of others, as true success. This mindset makes mentoring a foreign concept.

In coaching women to succeed, I am sometimes at a loss to figure out why many of us don't seek the skills of a mentor to help navigate the corporate arena. And surprisingly, those, who are mentored, describe their mentoring relationship as something that they did not actively seek. In most cases, the mentors sought them out instead and initiated the relationship.

In Pat Heim's book, Hardball For Women, she revealed that:

"Women often perceive mentors as unnecessary at best, and paternal at worst. They may think, 'I do good work. I'll be rewarded on my merit. Why do I need a mentor? What are they good for?' In eschewing an experienced advisor, not only do they miss the importance of interpersonal work for career advancement, but they remain ignorant of the rules of hardball being played around them."

Heim further states,

"Having a mentor may be more critical to a female's success than it is to her male colleagues."

The authors of Breaking the Glass Ceiling's extensive study of individuals who had made it to senior ranks of organizations found that only 38% of successful men had mentors. However, when it came to women executives, 100% had one. Therefore, mentors are indeed critical for women who are aiming to advance.

Waiting until you have developed a strong foundation creates the optimum time to seek mentorship because you and your mentor will see a return on the relationship much sooner.

Once you have the confidence, skills and solid reputation, mentors can help you navigate the corporate arena. They are great for providing feedback to help fine tune your skills as well.

A ROAST BEEF SANDWICH STORY

I used to pride myself for making it on my own, pulling myself up by my own bootstraps. For most of my career, I learned everything by myself and I didn't feel the need to receive help from anyone. My mother had made it

on her own and I wanted to follow in her footsteps. Seldom did I reach out to ask for advice or support. I wanted full credit for my success. I also didn't want to ask for help for fear that people wouldn't have the time or interest in supporting me. As an African American woman, I expected my career journey to be tough and I was up for the challenge.

Then one day, my ever-advancing career hit a roadblock. For the first time in my career, I was not performing well. My new boss was not pleased with my performance and I didn't know how to earn his respect. Although I was working my tail off, putting in 60+ hours a week, he did not see me as being productive. On top of that, our styles clashed and I was completely frustrated. I had never had a boss whom I could not win over. I prided myself on getting along with every personality and always made my bosses happy. However, this one in particular had me stumped.

Soon, I knew I was facing a career derailment. Struggling with how to work myself out of this situation, desperately I reached out to someone who I thought I could trust and someone who also knew my boss quite well. This action changed my career. Not only did this person help me see where I was going wrong, she also helped me understand my boss better and what he was looking for in me.

Having gone through something similar herself in the past, she was able to help me rethink how I was proving my worth. She also taught me about the importance of self-promotion and how to reestablish my relationship with my superior. She saved my career.

What I learned from that experience is that no one is an island and that the courage I had to ask for help showed how smart I was. My mentor told me, "Those who are smart enough to recognize the need for help and then seek out that help are the brilliant ones. It takes smarts to see what is wrong and seek to change it."

SELECTING AND OBTAINING MENTORS

According to *Harvard Business Review* in their 2010 article, *"Why Men Still Get More Promotions Than Women,"* mentors:

- ◎ Can sit at any level in the hierarchy
- ◎ Provide emotional support, feedback on how to improve, and other advice
- ◎ Serve as role models
- ◎ Help mentees' sense of competence and self-worth
- ◎ Focus on mentees' personal and professional development

Pat Heim in her book, *Hardball For Women*, whom I cited earlier, states that one should keep the following in mind when selecting mentors:

- It's better to have several.
- A man and a woman will have different strengths to offer.
- Choose someone highly respected, someone whom you admire.
- Your mentor's access to the dominant coalition can be critical.
- Ideally, you should feel comfortable with your mentor.
- His or her value system should be similar to yours.
- He or she should be willing to give you some time.
- You should be able to get insights from your mentor that you couldn't derive on your own.

Many professionals have the misguided belief that only seasoned executives make great mentors. Therefore, I tell many women to not overlook peers as potential mentors. I don't subscribe to that philosophy. I believe that you can find mentors at any level. When it comes to selecting mentors, I often remind women that they come in all shapes, sizes, colors, and most importantly, they can be found in every level within an organization. Selecting mentors is an art and you'll want to take many things into consideration when selecting yours such as:
- Compatibility
- Integrity
- Reputation
- Availability

If you happen to have a peer that is proficient in an area in which you are lacking, don't be afraid to seek their mentorship to help you in gaining proficiency in that area. I see this tactic work well when both parties engage in a reciprocal mentoring relationship where both benefit and they complement each other's strengths.

Talking about peers, I once gained mentorship from a peer who was excellent with numbers and maintained an airtight budget. She could account for every dime her department spent. She took accounting to a whole new level of trending, forecasting and the like. I was in awe of her financial knowledge and her accounting skills. I, on the other hand, hated dealing with the numbers. Consequently, managing my budget was torture and I struggled with understanding what the numbers were telling me.

After countless attempts to get my budget under control, I approached her and asked if she'd teach me how to manage my budget better. She was open to doing it, but made it known that she didn't want to waste her time if I wasn't serious about learning. Reaching out to my peer was the best thing that could have happened to me that year. She took me under her wing and showed me simple ways to manage my budget, the difference between reporting elements and how to present metrics. She increased my financial acumen. Before I knew it, I faced my budget with confidence, could anticipate trends and was forecasting like a true accountant, a skill I knew would impress my boss and benefit my career for years to come.

The best part of this peer mentoring was my ability to assist her as well. Although she was a wiz at numbers, her interpersonal skills were appalling. Her sharp tongue left her subordinates cut to shreds and she often left a trail of dead bodies wherever she went. Once we established a trusting relationship, she asked for my assistance with retaining her staff. Having noticed that I was not having the amount of turnover she was, I was able to help her build effective relationships with her peers and team. She was forever thankful.

Our mentoring relationship worked out well. Although we never thought about it as such, we entered into "reciprocal mentoring." She helped me with my budgeting and I helped her improve her interpersonal skills. It was a win-win situation all around.

Another good way to obtain a mentor is to give something first. Offer to help a potential mentor before seeking their help. Reciprocity in mentoring is important. Many mentees think of only taking from the relationship. The best mentoring relationships pay back when both parties get something from the engagement.

When it comes to mentoring, it is also important to obtain mentors from both inside and outside of your organization. Mentors from the inside of the organization may assist you with your organization's politics and help you in avoiding pitfalls. They can educate you regarding your organization's hidden culture, the unspoken rules and the high stake politics. They can also provide you with a supportive network that could help arm you against adversaries.

External mentors are also beneficial. They are great resources that help provide an outside/neutral perspective. These internal and external perspectives provide you with well-rounded support.

OTHER ADVICE AND LESSONS LEARNED

Karen Williams who is the executive chef of the chapter on strategy and execution shared with me her thoughts on mentoring:

"When it comes to mentors, I made the mistake of asking people to mentor me who may not have had the time or interest. This caused the relationship to be forced. Most beneficial mentoring relationships happen naturally. Most people don't understand that it is the mentee who drives the mentoring relationship. They are responsible for keeping the relationship going and determining what comes out of it.

It is also important to broaden your perspective of who your mentors are in your life. There are mentors for every occasion. There are mentors such as those who will give you a kick in the pants when needed, those who will encourage you to take risks, and some who will tell you when to put on you "big girl panties."

THE RISK OF HAVING A MALE MENTOR

First let me start off by saying many women have been very successful with male mentors. I have certainly benefitted from several. In fact, having access to a male mentor will give you a balanced perspective on the politics in the workplace. Also, since there are far more male senior professionals, it may be unrealistic to limit yourself to just female mentors. However, that being said for women, there is a slight risk in having male mentors that should be mentioned.

I have heard of a few challenging experiences women have had with their male mentors. Although some of the mentoring relationships started out on a promising note, as they progressed, things got tricky. At times, these women felt that the relationship could only go just so far until things started to feel awkward between them. These women believed that their attractiveness, age, or being single tended to get in the way and often took the relationship from mentoring to flirting. To tell the truth, I was a little embarrassed to bring this issue up, as were most of the women who mentioned it to me. The truth is, many women often struggle with their working relationship with men. And to be fair, men have also felt uncomfortable mentoring young and attractive women as well.

In my own experiences over the years, a few of my male mentors actually pulled away from me after awhile because they felt uncomfortable about what others may think, even though we were always very professional in our interactions. Many of them were open about their feelings and told me that although they were supportive of my development, they had to advise me from afar.

Unfortunately, some people have a difficult time separating professional/personal relationships when they see a woman and a man spending time together. Although you may have remained strictly professional, people may still be skeptical. This doesn't mean that you should not seek a male mentor. Just make an extra effort to look and act professional at all times. Women, although we hate to admit it, are under a different level of scrutiny and, double standards do still exist. If people "talk," it is always the woman who will get the stigma.

DIFFERENCE BETWEEN SPONSORS AND MENTORS

Many say that women are over- mentored and under-sponsored. According to the *Harvard Business Review* article, "Why Men Still Get More Promotions Than Women," compared to men, more women have mentors, (83% compared to 76% of men). However, fewer women have sponsors. Experts say that sponsorship is a key ingredient to make it to the top ranks.

Many people confuse mentorship with sponsorship. A mentor is someone who provides feedback and advice. A sponsor, on the other hand, goes beyond just feedback and advice. They also use their influence, clout and power to advocate for you and remove barriers and expose you to influential people in their network.

More women are lacking this sponsorship and it dramatically affects their career advancement. Sponsors can help take your career to a whole new level.

Guidelines to effective sponsorships as outlined in the above article, states that all sponsors must fit the following criteria:

- Must be senior managers with influence
- Give protégée exposure to other executives who may help their careers
- Make sure their people are considered for promising opportunities and challenging assignments
- Protect their protégés from negative publicity or damaging contact with senior executives
- Fight to get their people promoted

In order to excel through your organization, you need to have influential people promoting you for high-level positions. Because women tend not to have sponsors backing them up, they are considered too risky for high-level roles. No one is advocating and building trust that they can do the job. You see this often in organizations where women are seeking promotional opportunities. If a woman is unsponsored, it is difficult to get higher ups to believe that she can handle the job. Many women have to leave their organizations, often going to competitors just to get higher-level jobs. Those who do make it up the ranks, you can guarantee that there is a sponsor somewhere advocating for them.

If you want to know how well an organization does with sponsoring women, just look at where their high-level female executives come from. If the majority of them came from outside the organization, it is a sure sign that the women within the organization are lacking the key ingredient of sponsorship.

FORMAL MENTORING PROGRAMS

Studies show that women are promoted two-three times more in companies with formal mentoring programs. Organizations that have formal mentoring programs are good for women because they usually involve a strategic matching process and connect women to influential networks of top executives and those who have been successful in the organization. Women who have participated in such programs are usually followed throughout their time with the company and their progress is continuously evaluated. Through this process, barriers are eliminated and high-potential women are supported and sponsored.

Organizations committed to the mentorship of women through formal programs, usually are better equipped to identify barriers that prevent women from moving forward. I always advise women who are considering joining a company with a formal mentoring program in place to seize the opportunity.

Mentors and sponsors are critical to your success. Be sure to surround yourself with mentors inside and outside your organization. Think outside the box and you may find a good one in a peer as well.

Extra Toppings
to Enhance
Your Sandwich

◎ Don't overlook peers
◎ Look for formal mentoring programs
◎ Don't make yourself an island
◎ You must seek sponsorship
◎ Diversify and broaden your network

chapter ten

Sure-fire Ingredient #7
Effective Relationships

"The ability to build strong and affirming relationships is perhaps the most critical to overall career success."
-Jocelyn

EXECUTIVE CHEF

Gerard Van Grinsven | President & CEO, Henry Ford West Bloomfield Hospital, Michigan

A Passionate Discussion on Effective Relationships with Gerard Van Grinsven, President & CEO, Henry Ford West Bloomfield Hospital

"Leaders, who don't see the importance of relationships as an important element of their success, struggle. They believe their struggle is due to their lack of knowledge or technical skills. They also believe that

*those attributes will help them obtain buy in or support.
This is a common misconception among leaders."*
-Gerard Van Grinsven

*At the time Gerard was hired as the CEO for
Henry Ford West Bloomfield Hospital, I was leading
our executive recruitment and assimilation efforts.
His ability to build relationships with customers and
the community was a well-known talent. Soon
the buzz of Gerard and his exceptional talent got
around and everyone was talking about him.*

*Gerard and I shared similar backgrounds and
each have a passion for people. Both previously
from the hospitality industry, we grew up around
service, guest relations and generating a culture
focused on talent. Therefore, when we officially
met at his welcome reception, we instantly
connected. Surprisingly, I found myself a
member of Gerard's executive team 10 months
later as his vice president of talent and workforce
strategies.*

*Working with Gerard was fascinating. His
vision, understanding of leadership and most
importantly his ability to build and enhance
relationships is exceptional. Together, we
focused on building a talent-based organization
and set the groundwork for a recruitment process
to select and retain top talent. Our goal was to
select talent with potential to build exceptional
relationships with our patients, their families and
the community.*

Through his leadership and mentorship, I learned the importance of relationships and how they play a major role in one's career. His charismatic nature made him a joy to engage with and it also earned him "rock star" status among health care CEO's. Through his vision, leadership and courage, he helped take "health and healing beyond the boundaries of the imagination."

GERARD'S CAREER JOURNEY

With more than 24 years of global experience in the luxury hospitality industry, Gerard Van Grinsven was asked to bring his innovative approaches and expertise in service excellence to the world of health care. In 2006, he was named president and chief executive officer of the 300-bed, $360 million Henry Ford West Bloomfield Hospital.

Prior to joining Henry Ford, he served as vice president and area general manager for The Ritz-Carlton Hotel Company in Dearborn and as vice president and area general manager of The Ritz-Carlton hotels in Cleveland, St. Louis and Philadelphia.

Gerard's vision is for Henry Ford West Bloomfield Hospital to be embraced as both a community center for well-being and a cutting-edge hospital. In addition to state-of-the-art equipment and the best clinical practices, the hospital features a wellness center, a healthy restaurant and other unique features including a pond and landscaped courtyards that contribute to a healing environment.

Gerard's approach focuses on a passion for superior service, a total commitment to creating an environment of excellence and building successful relationships with the community, patients and employees.

During his career, he has opened 20 Ritz-Carlton properties worldwide. He was a key member of the team responsible for the company winning the prestigious Malcolm Baldrige National Quality Award in 1999. He executed The Ritz-Carlton Re-Born project, which resulted in The Ritz-Carlton in Dearborn being the #1 hotel in the company for improved guest and employee satisfaction scores. Van Grinsven also has served on the HFHS Western Wayne/Downriver Board of Trustees.

Gerard holds a Bachelor of Arts degree in Hotel Management from The Hotel Management School, Maastricht, The Netherlands. He is a former board member of the Detroit Regional Chamber and the Michigan Kidney Foundation. In 2003, the Detroit Regional Chamber named him one of the "100 Emerging Business Leaders."

GERARD'S PERSPECTIVE ON RELATIONSHIPS
(in his words)

"We are not in the business of health care but in the business of relationships. If we treat our people in a valuable manner, they will not want to go somewhere else. People want to do business with those whom they like."

-Gerard Van Grinsven

Let me give you an example of how I feel about meaningful relationships. The first day I arrived as the general manager of Ritz Carlton in Dearborn, Michigan, I got 120 emails. Most of the emails were not meant for me. I was just copied so that individuals could cover themselves, or leverage my name. What I discovered was that the people were not personally communicating to each other, thus they were not accustom to having meaningful relationships.

Therefore, I put an end to emails unless it was a matter of life or death. Emails prevent you from having a personal relationship with guests and your colleagues. Because many were too busy focusing on covering their butts, we had the lowest guest engagement scores in the company. Therefore, I set out to refocus our priorities.

When it comes to organizations, you hurt yourself by having a "meeting culture." Instead of being in meetings all day, leaders should spend their time building relationships with the customer. Customers need to see us, interact with us and get to know us. This makes them feel valued. When you make others feel valued, not only do you build loyalty, you feel valued as well.

Most of us need a human connection and an emotional connection. We want to feel touched and cared for. The successful leaders of the future understand that a culture that is all about relationships is sure-fire. Some people are naturally talented to build relationships. These natural talents don't change much over the years.

One would say I was naturally talented in relationship building from my early years. Since the young age of four years old, my aunts told me that I was always the first to answer the door when the doorbell rang. I would eagerly greet our guests. If building relationships is not one of your strong talents, and it is important to you, then you must work to develop it.

I am a strong believer that when you break bread with someone, the relationship changes. It means more than when you just meet with someone in an office. When you break bread, you change the environment.

People are more apt to open up about their feelings, desires and fears in these types of casual settings.

In my position at Henry Ford West Bloomfield Hospital, I spent six months going to the homes of different diverse groups within our community. I went without an agenda. I wanted to get to know the people. When I started to eat bread or food with my community, then I was treated as a member of the family. They opened up and shared more insights and we had meaningful conversations.

When it comes to relationships, women are more apt to create relationships than men. Generally speaking, it comes more natural to women. In today's business environment, women are so important. Women have tremendous power when it comes to purchasing. Many organizations don't realize that.

Although I did not have a health care background when hired for the president and CEO position at Henry Ford West Bloomfield Hospital, I was hired because I was viewed as someone who was talented at establishing relationships. I am confident that our CEO, Nancy Schlichting knew I could overcome the lack of experience and excel due to my ability to create meaningful relationships.

I invested a lot time in establishing relationships with key leaders even with those whom were tough on me due to my inexperience. I made a conscious effort to break down barriers and break the ice. This helped me to be successful.

If I were to give you three tips on how to boost your relationship skills, they would be as follows:

1. **Be vulnerable:** Let people see that you are human. You might have a big title, but you are still human. Don't be afraid to show that to people. Leaders sometime believe that they have to be superhuman with all the answers and be perfect. Sometimes it is okay to share with your people and tell them that you are worried or to apologize when wrong. Admit a fault. This is powerful and sends a strong message to your people. Let people know that you are real.

2. **Be honest.** Don't hint around the surface. Don't worry too much about whether you are going to hurt

others. When people know you are sincere, you can tell it like you feel it. People will respect that you are honest about your feelings.

3. Be critical, and embrace emotional intelligence. Get to know yourself better. There are many leaders whom are not truthful to themselves. They keep trying to be somebody whom they are not. You might find things about you that might help you continue to grow. So many leaders have been conditioned to be a certain way. They may not be happy at where they are. Not because of what they want, but what others have told them to be. Once you know more about yourself, you can be better at leadership.

GERARD'S OTHER LESSONS LEARNED AND ADVICE

I don't see women being valued in the workplace like they should. Women need to understand what is most important to them, what their talents are, no matter what others say and have faith that if you focus on those talents, you will be successful. You must ask yourself, am I willing to be fully faithful to myself in what really makes me tick? When you are doing what you are passionate about, it makes you attractive. People want to be around people who know where they are going. Things will come to you, like jobs, contacts, etc.

If you connect with your natural talents, you will overcome all of the hurdles. You have to have the confidence that says, "I can do this." Connect with yourself. Once you do this, you will become more successful in your work and relationships.

It is crucial to take charge of your destiny. Often women have to make sacrifices for their family, parents, husbands and etc. Then one day they wake up and they don't know who they are any longer.

Even when you have established a path to your destiny, at times you will have to divert due to bad weather. However, if you are the one in charge, you have charge of your destiny. It is those, who don't have the confidence to take charge of their destiny, and

when they have detours, they get taken off course.
It is important to define who am I, what is important to me. This tells you how you will approach your relationships with your family, career and community.
You must learn to make others feel valued in relationships to make a difference.

THE IMPORTANCE OF EFFECTIVE RELATIONSHIPS

The ability to build strong and affirming relationships is perhaps the most critical to overall success in any career. It is the effective relationships you establish that will open doors for you. These are the relationships that not only enhance your reputation; these relationships can save you from some impending disaster on the horizon.

Most successful executives, attribute their success to having great relationships. Many of them devote up to 60% of their time cultivating them. Compared to women, research shows that men spend up to three times more time than women cultivating relationships and networking in the workplace. When I read that, I found it ironic since women are said to be social beings. You would think we would network more than men. Once at one of my workshops, a woman challenged me by saying that, "In my office, women socialized more than the men. Therefore, women do network more," she asserted.

Now don't get me wrong, we do talk more than men in the workplace. However, don't confuse socializing with networking. Talking helps us build relationships, but not necessarily the types of strategic relationships and connections that will make a difference in our careers.

John C. Maxwell, in his book, *Talent is Never Enough*, starts out a chapter with John Wooden's impressive words from Wooden's book, *My Personal Best,*

"Nothing will influence your talent as much as the important relationships in your life. Surround yourself with people who add value to you and encourage you, and your talent will go in a positive direction. Spend time with people who constantly drain you, pull you in the wrong direction, or try to knock you down, and it will be almost impossible for your talent to take flight. People can trace the successes and failures in their lives to their most significant relationships."

When it comes to building relationships, men are more likely than women to get out of their offices frequently to go to breakfast, lunch, and dinner or for drinks with key colleagues, superiors and leaders. They are also more likely to meet up to watch and/or play sports together. At the age of 22, my stepfather took up golf simply because he realized that all the important business within his organization was being conducted between the men who routinely got together on the golf course. When he recognized this, he immediately took golfing lessons and before long he was playing golf with the "big wig" guys. He swears to this day that he would have never advanced as far in his career without the relationships he built on the golf course.

Another interesting thing about the difference between men and women is that men seldom talk "shop" when they get together. When men get together, they don't solve world peace, they don't try to impress, instead they just bond.

Women, on the other hand, usually talk about work when we network. Whenever we are out with other professionals, especially with those from our organization, we can't resist the urge to talk about work. If we aren't talking about the actual work, you can bet your last dollar, we are talking about the people (who are not out with us, mind you) with whom we work.

Many of us believe that the only thing that connects us one to the other is our work. We fail to shape the relationships we have with other professionals around other interests. If we could learn to develop relationships with each other separate from the job and truly connect, we would then be in a better position to bond together. Bonding happens when people establish common ground. It is in relationships where people bond, that help careers.

We also spend a lot of time at our desks. If you walk down the hall in most organizations, you will find women leaders in their offices with their nose to the grindstone. I know I had my share of doing the same. We are hard workers, trying to get it all done. We believe that "getting it done, being available and supporting our team" is the key to our success. We believe that this practice shows dedication and commitment. However, the message it sends is that we are not interested in being part of the team, and that we would rather function in isolation.

If you want to reach the executive ranks of the C-suite, you must get out of the office, move around and start building strong relationships with key people. Building effective relationships with people both inside and outside your organization is critical. The power of strong relationships cannot be overstated. Relationships are what make you well known within your organization and other networking circuits. When you are unseen, you are out of mind.

Building relationships takes energy. And believe me, this is another good reason to be sure to get work done through others, so you may reserve your energy for relationship building.

MINORITY WOMEN MUST WORK HARDER TO BUILD RELATIONSHIPS IN THE WORKPLACE

When it comes to building relationships in the workplace, minority women build relationships differently than non-minorities. Please know I am not bringing up race to talk about how it is harder for minority women in the workplace (although research says it is). I bring it up, because I care about women as a whole, period. And, because I believe that if we stick together and make it work for us collectively, then we will make more progress, than if we work separately. There is indeed strength in numbers.

Now, when I say there is strength in numbers, as many others have said, this is what goes through my head:

In 2010, women represented 46.7% of the workforce overall. Of that 46.7%, 12% (6,114,000) are minority women. Can you imagine what could happen if we work together as a collective force? That way we could leverage our power representing almost half of the workforce.

It is the collective force that has helped men all along. As a whole, men fair better than women in the workplace. What If we work to do the same?

WHY DIVERSE WOMEN HAVE TO WORK HARDER ON BUILDING RELATIONSHIPS

According to *Catalyst* in the article titled, "Building Trust, Between Managers and Diverse Women Direct Reports" by Giscmbe, Agin, Deva,

"Diverse women, (Diverse women, defined as those belonging to racial minority groups in North America), often face greater challenges than white women in forming trusting relationships at work. Negative stereotyping, exclusion from influential networks and difficulty in gaining access to high visibility assignments can influence the ways in which diverse women experience workplaces, and can limit diverse women's access to trusting relationships."

The *Catalyst* report refrained from subjective comparisons. Instead it focused strictly on statistics on how each gender and minority group faired in the workplace. The study encouragingly showed that white males actually are acting on behalf of their female direct reports regardless of the women's racial background.

Catalyst called this act *reliance* which is one of the two critical ingredients for a trusting relationship.

This *reliance* is great for women, as it means we are halfway there. However, the study did find a major difference in the way "reliance" relates to how minority women view this support in terms of it increasing their opportunity for advancement. In other words, although both white and minority women were equal in terms of having reliance with their supervisor, white women were more likely to feel that this "reliance" would get them more advancement opportunities. Whereas, minority women didn't necessary believe it would help them advance.

Catalyst attributes this difference in expectation to diverse women's experiences in the workplace. Diverse women tend to find the workplace as more exclusive than white women. They perceive their experience to include negative stereotyping and reported that they perceived more racism, sexism and double standards. *Catalyst* adds that, negative stereotyping is damaging and limits advancement opportunities for minority women.

It appears that diverse women know that although they may have their supervisor's reliance, they may not be able to overcome the stereotypes that portray them as, *"lacking qualities commonly associated with effective leadership."*

This discrepancy is believed by *Catalyst*, to be attributed to lower levels of the second important ingredient to building relationships, *disclosure*. Disclosure is described as -

"Occurring when direct reports communicate sensitive or personal information to a manager."

Diverse women consistently have lower ratings of disclosure when it comes to relationships with their managers. Relationships lacking disclosure can jeopardize development, the ability to build trust and ultimately a sound relationship. It is the combination of the managers' lack of awareness on how to address differing cultures and the diverse woman's lack of feeling safe to disclose personal or sensitive information (including performance issues) that contributes to this dillemna.

According to the study, the deeper the level of disclosure, the deeper the trust, and thus a stronger relationship. The stronger the relationship between those with higher reliance and disclosure, the more women reported confidence in career advancement opportunities.

When it comes to disclosure, personal and sensitive information according to the report, includes sharing things such as:

- Communicating about a mistake
- Asking for assistance
- Requesting support or resources

WHAT DIVERSE WOMEN MUST DO DIFFERENTLY

It is recommended that diverse women make a stronger effort to initiate the disclosure part of the relationship with their supervisor. Being a diverse woman myself, I know how challenging this can be. Culturally we are more reserved and private. Also, we often feel as though in order to combat negative stereotypes or perceived double standards, we have to appear competent. Therefore, we are less likely to disclose the need for help, support or resources. It feels too risky.

If you wish to have a stronger relationship with your supervisor, you will have to work through your natural tendencies or reservations by taking steps to share first. Chances are your supervisor is waiting for you to make the first step or set the tone. Start by asking for feedback on your performance or sharing your career ambitions. If you are reserved with your manager, you are probably going to get the same response in return. It may be that they are trying to avoid making you feel uncomfortable. If you let them know it is okay to take the relationship deeper, then they may follow your lead.

Overall, relationships are critical to career success. It is important to build and sustain them within your organization and externally in your networking community. Invest in relationships by breaking bread, making others feel valued and eliminating barriers. Get out of your office and start building those relationships.

Extra Toppings
to Enhance
Your Sandwich

- ◎ Spend time building relationships
- ◎ Be strategic in your approach
- ◎ Support all women in the relationship building process
- ◎ Use social/ casual settings to break down walls
- ◎ Be authentic

chapter eleven

Sure-fire Ingredient #8
Effective Communication

" In as brief as six seconds, others get an impression of you based on what you communicate. We must master the art of communicating confidently to remain competitive." -Jocelyn

EXECUTIVE CHEF

Denise Ilitch | President, Ilitch Enterprises, Inc.

A Thought-Provoking Discussion on Effective Communication with Denise Ilitch, President, Ilitch Enterprises, Inc.

"Effective communication is about speaking in plain English and understanding to whom you are communicating. You must learn to say exactly what you mean and keep it very simple. What can be said in three seconds, but actually said in 60, can cause you to lose the reader or listener."-Denise Ilitch

169

The community knows Denise for her demonstrated commitment. Being aware of her commitment to the advancement of women, I was honored to meet her in person at the 2010, "Remarkable Women's Luncheon." Hosted by Florine Mark, founder of Weight Watchers of America, in Michigan, Denise was a featured speaker.

She spoke about the importance of communicating with confidence and after the lunch, we walked out together and struck up a conversation. Together we stood in the parking lot talking about the importance of giving back to the community of women. Our common ground was a similar passion and commitment.

Denise departed by giving me her business card, and encouraging me to continue my work. I promised to keep her posted on my status. She also offered to assist with promoting my book as a gesture to give back to local authors. Furthermore, she agreed to an interview. I called on Denise to share what she had learned in her career on the importance of effective communication. Here's her story…

DENISE'S CAREER JOURNEY

Denise received her B.A. degree from the University of Michigan in 1977 and her J.D. degree from the University of Detroit in 1980. She shared that education has always been important to her. Currently, Denise is the president of Ilitch Enterprises, owner of Denise Ilitch Designs, and the owner and publisher of *Ambassador Magazine*, a leading Detroit lifestyle magazine she started with Dennis Archer, Jr., the son of former Detroit mayor, Dennis Archer. Denise is also "of counsel" at Clark Hill PLC, where she advises clients in the areas of business practice, corporate law and government policy.

Prior to joining Clark Hill, Denise Ilitch was the president of Ilitch Holdings, Inc., a privately held business that manages Little Caesars Enterprises, the Detroit Red Wings, the Detroit Tigers, and Olympia Entertainment. In support of her efforts to enhance educational opportunities, she established the *Denise Ilitch Scholarship for Women* at Walsh College and serves as a Distinguished Visiting Business Executive at Detroit Mercy School of Law.

She has served on the board of the Detroit Branch of the NAACP, was a Detroit Red Wings Alternate Governor for the National Hockey League, and was a board member of Major League Baseball. She has received the B'nai B'rith International Great American Traditions Award, the Clara Barton Award from the American Red Cross, and was named 2007 Alumnus of the Year by the University of Detroit Mercy Law School. Denise is also a regular panelist on the CBS - TV show, *Michigan Matters*.

Denise spent 30 years growing her family's business. When she originally joined the family business, they had 50 Little Caesars stores. Today, Little Caesars has grown to almost 5,000 stores. Her professional journey followed the growth of the family business. She started her career in the legal profession, but eventually fell in love with marketing.

Just by chance, the marketing department was right next door to the legal department. Denise stated that the marketing people would often come over to legal for approval on ads from a trademark perspective. However, instead of just giving legal advice, Denise found herself giving input on the designs and promotions as well.

Her suggestions were often creative and thus adopted. Her ideas increased sales when they were incorporated. It didn't take long before she decided that marketing was the place for her. Once she aligned her work with her passion, her career took off.

Denise is the oldest of the seven Ilitch children and daughter of Michael and Marian Bayoff Ilitch. Michael "Mike" Ilitch, Sr. (born Michael Ilievski, 1929) is an entrepreneur and also the owner of the Detroit Red Wings, and the Detroit Tigers. In addition to his sports ownerships, he is the founder and owner of Little Caesars Pizza, which, since 1959, has become an international fast food franchise.

Mike Ilitch has been at the center of Detroit's downtown redevelopment efforts since he purchased and renovated the Fox Theatre and relocated his headquarters into its offices. He is a first generation American of Macedonian decent.

In 2000, they appointed two of their children, Denise and her brother, Christopher, co-presidents of Ilitch Holdings, Inc. Christopher Ilitch was named to the new post of president and CEO.

Denise eventually left the privately held company to start her own Ilitch Enterprises.

DENISE'S PERSPECTIVE ON EFFECTIVE COMMUNICATION
(in her words)

Depending on what role you play, communication is key. For instance, if I am a practicing lawyer, it is important that I communicate as an advocate for the person I am representing. As a publisher, it is important to communicate effectively to the reader.

Having a law degree really improved my skills in communication. It teaches you how to articulate an issue, how to craft an argument, advocate for a position, and stand pact when challenged. It also taught me not to be intimidated when challenged. I learned to think logically and to assess a situation from all sides. This ability to communicate effectively has contributed to the success of my career.

When you are able to communicate well, people understand where you are coming from. This decreases miscommunication. If you are capable of communicating with all different audiences, this also can help advance one's career.

Running a large organization has helped me realize the importance of communication. Never have I heard anyone say, "Boy they sure over communicate." Communicating is challenging. People hear things differently. Also, what you think you are saying and what people hear are often very different.

An important part of communicating is listening. Listening is an active act just as speaking is. Some people have poor listening skills. When you stop listening you can become insular or closed to all levels of input, and that can become a problem. Some leaders stop listening and surround themselves with others who are like them and tell them what they want to hear.

Sometimes people think communicating is about verbalizing what they think. Ariana Huffington, creator of the Huffington Post, is a role model for me in terms of communication. Also, Carol Goss, CEO of the Skillman Foundation in which I am a trustee, is a great communicator.

Practice is important when it comes to communicating. Remember to practice listening, and push yourself out of your comfort zone. Speak as much as you can and if you are interested in writing, take lessons and write often to increase your vocabulary and education. If you have to advocate for a position as a lawyer, there is a lot of practice involved in that. If you are a CEO and you have to make a presentation to your team, practice is important.

Although I don't see many differences when it comes to genders, men tend to be more direct in their communication with less emotion. When one is an effective communicator, it doesn't matter what your gender is. Most just have different styles.

Communication is key in all aspects of one's life. It is critical as a parent, a spouse, a daughter and the success of one's life. Communication is critical for all the different roles in your life, not just business.

In our magazine, The Ambassador, we talk about what is happening around town, we talked about trends, and we talk about fashion. But we also choose to talk about individuals who are doing great things in the community. We aim to inspire and motivate. That is a very important value. We like to influence in a positive way and show a positive angle. We don't tear people down, we build people up.

HOW DO YOU COMMUNICATE?

Ask yourself...

When you enter a room, do you …

- ◎ Command respect?
- ◎ Engage others?
- ◎ Leave a lasting impression?
- ◎ Demonstrate confidence and power?

Early on, I used to think I was a great communicator until I answered those questions. Because I did a lot of presentations, I assumed my communication skills were sufficient. However, I realized I couldn't say "yes" to commanding respect and demonstrating power when I spoke.

For most women, when we think about communication, we think solely about the words that we speak. Many women ask me to help them speak with "power words." I just cringe when I see a woman who wishes to learn to speak powerfully, when in fact she is sending a weak message nonverbally.

A weak message has nothing to do with spoken words; it is all about what you are saying nonverbally through your body language, tone and gestures. Nonverbal cues such as, posture, expressions and eye contact, send messages that can make or break hiring decisions, business deals and a person's credibility.

In as brief as six seconds, you communicate your level of confidence, authority, competence and more, all without even opening your mouth. Women today, must master the art of confident body language to maintain their competitive edge. Mastering the art starts with understanding the fundamentals of how you send messages and how they are being perceived.

Surprisingly, 55% of communication comes from your nonverbal cues. An additional 38% of communication comes from the tone, pitch and pace of your voice. Therefore, a staggering 93% of your communication effectiveness has little to do with the words that you speak. When you understand that ninety-three percent of how you communicate is nonverbal, it becomes clear that you must work on the ninety-three percent to be effective.

THE POWER OF FIRST IMPRESSIONS

To understand the power of nonverbal communication consider how powerful first impressions are to perceptions. A great exercise I ask women to try is...when at a meeting, networking or business function complete the following steps:

Step 1. Make a list of descriptive words that highlight first impressions of someone in the room.

Step 2. Next to each description, write the reason you have that impression. For example, a first impression description may be "boredom." Therefore, your reason may be that the person is fidgeting in their seat and yawning a great deal.

Often those who try this exercise, find that the majority of their observations had little to do verbal communication. Most of what their descriptions were based on had to do with nonverbal communication.

To enhance your communication effectiveness, focusing on your nonverbal communication is important. Understanding this will do more for your communication skills than all the power words in the world.

FIRST IMPRESSIONS: THE **P**OWERFUL **S**IX **S**ECONDS* **(PSS)**

Without ever opening your mouth to speak, within six seconds you have communicated your level of…

- confidence
- intelligence
- knowledge
- risk-taking
- professionalism
- value
- honesty

- credibility
- trust
- stamina
- creativity
- health
- potential
- leadership

*© 2010, SASHE, LLC

The above list could go on and on. The PSS leads to the first impression. *"You only have one chance to make a first impression."* PSS is all about that one opportunity to start on a powerful footing.

According to Deborah Williams, senior vice president of human resources at Parkview Health in Indiana,

"The first impression we make is the one that shapes the entire interaction we have with other individuals. It helps people decide if they are going to resonate with what you have to say. The most important thing is to be comfortable and to focus on what is going to present the best of "you" instead of trying to impersonate someone else. Always be professional - and that is relative - but in a way that is authentic to you. When I interact with others whom I haven't had a lot

of exposure to, I do a lot of listening upfront. Paying attention to their body language and what they say. This helps me deliver my information to them in a way that they can receive. I also like to engage in a lot of lively dialogue. However, some individuals are not interested in dialogue. Therefore, it is important to be observant to gage the style of the individuals who you are trying to influence or engage."

The following steps will help you make a PSS:

STEP 1: Determine what type of impression you want to make

Many women fail to take this important step. We assume that we know what message we wish to send and to whom. Many of us fail to flex our communication style for the different situations we encounter. It is to your advantage to determine if you are communicating the right message to the right audience. Do you need to show strength, knowledge, teamwork, leadership, or empathy? You must first decide what you wish to convey, before you can determine how to do it.

STEP 2: Determine how you are going to communicate that message nonverbally

Your first impression is mainly based on the following criteria:

- ◎ Your appearance
- ◎ Your posture
- ◎ Your facial expressions
- ◎ Your greeting

These are the four areas addressed during my coaching sessions.

APPEARANCE

Feeling good about how you look is critical in looking confident. If you don't like how you look, it comes across in your body language. Women underestimate how that affects sending confident messages. You can always tell when a woman is uncomfortable about her appearance. However, a woman who is comfortable with it, leaves a positive impression.

POSTURE

Our mothers were right when they told us to, "Stand up straight, hold our head high and to tuck our chins in." Good posture speaks confidence especially standing tall. Much research supports the fact that people perceive taller people to be leaders and self-starters. It is this reason that the majority of CEO's are over six feet tall.

Height is important and I always tell women to heightened themselves as much as possible. Tall people are perceived as stronger leaders, more influential, confident and capable.

In the 2009 article, *"Tall People Earn More; Height, Leadership and Persuasion Abilities"* by Cheryn Tan, the comparison is made between the success of tall people verses short people. According to their findings, taller people are generally more successful than their shorter counterparts.

The link between height and leadership is said to be unconscious on our part and can be traced back to early human history. According to psychologist Timothy Judge, from the University of Florida, leadership qualities are ascribed to taller people because they were believed to be more capable of protecting the tribe (they could see danger coming); and even after millennia of evolution, the same belief has remained intact within our society today.

Literally and figuratively, height allows one to look imperiously down upon others, which could give one a towering sense of confidence. The logical explanation is that tall people have been believed to become greater leaders; hence they naturally step into those positions and gradually improve their people skills.

It is arguable whether this is a case of a self-fulfilling prophecy – do tall people naturally have higher self-esteem or is it only so because of the way they are perceived? Nevertheless, this increased confidence has yielded positive benefits for the non-vertically challenged. A 2004 study published in the *Journal of Applied Psychology* suggested that taller people could earn up to $789 more per year than shorter people (tall, being defined as: above 5'9" for men and above 5'3" for women).

For women who are "vertically challenged," heightening may be done in a variety of ways such as: *Heels, good posture, raising your chair, holding head up, raise your hair (be careful here, no beehives!), wearing solid colors or tone-on-tone, vertical pinstripes.*

FACIAL EXPRESSIONS

When it comes to communication, the face tells it all. It often amazes me the various facial expressions I see in meetings. I see dislike, boredom, admiration, confusion, disbelief, disgust, anger, etc. on the faces of professionals everyday. Most of the times many of us are unaware of what we are communicating through these expressions.

Facial expressions are an important part of body language. In terms of expressions, smiles are generally recognized as friendly and trustworthy in most cultures. Good eye contact, but not forced is also seen as positive in establishing rapport, respect and trust (with the exception of some cultures).

Being aware of what your face is saying is important in ensuring that you are sending the message you wish to send.

GREETINGS

Greetings are important. Usually when you are making your first impression. It is during this time that we communicate confidence, competency and trust. The next five steps are things I learned along the way that have helped me make the right impression:

1. Walk tall
2. Initiate introductions with a firm handshake, eye contact and a smile
3. Don't rush to sit. Be the last person standing.
4. Keep hands open with palms up as much as possible
5. Show energy

If you are uncomfortable speaking in front of people, began to develop your level of ease by first talking more in small group settings at work. When you've develop ease in talking in meetings, volunteer for speaking engagements either at your church, women's group or other settings. A good way to evaluate how well you're doing is to bring someone you respect and trust to hear you speak. Having them critique you will allow you to know how well you present and where you need to improve.

There are many excellent training materials to help you communicate well. I recommend:

1. Dale Carnegie Leadership Training
2. Selfgrowth.com
3. National Seminars Training
4. Toast Masters International
5. My workbook, *How to Communicate with Confidence*

(You may find it at www.jocelyngiangradne.com)

Another way to improve your speaking is by watching and listening to the great speakers. While driving alone, listen to a well-known orator; listen to great audio books; or study various training on effective communication styles. One of the greatest trainings I've come across is Norman Vincent Peals' *How to Make Friends and Influence Others*. It is a classic and offers effective methods on how to engage others and increase your communication skills.

CONNECTING WITH YOUR AUDIENCE IS IMPORTANT IN COMMUNICATION

In our quest to communicate, sometimes we fail to consider the language of the audience. This is especially true when we are passionate about our topic. We focus more on getting our message out instead of thinking about what the audience wants to hear.

Understanding and connecting to your audience is important to engaging listeners. There are many ways to help you do this. The three steps I use are:

STEP 1. Know as much as you can about your audience. *I do what I can to know my audience beforehand. I try to obtain information such as their goals, hot buttons, fears, problems, style, preferences, culture, rules, leaders (informal/formal), etc.*

STEP 2. Speak their language. Knowing the terminology, jargon and acronyms used by your audience builds credibility and trust. When you speak the same language, they will see you as an insider.

Audiences like insiders and view them positively. Many women rate themselves low in business acumen. It is important to enhance your business lingo. Mentors are great for helping you grow this skill.

STEP 3. Conduct pulse checks. Survey your audience periodically throughout your communication. Span the room and determine if your points are getting across and whether people are bored. You can determine how things are going by looking at the nonverbal signals of your audience.

A CORN BEEF ON RYE SANDWICH STORY

My best lesson in effective communication came from a former senior executive, at Henry Ford Health System in Detroit, Michigan.

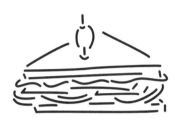

During our annual update meeting, he gave me a lesson that improved my skill level significantly in communicating effectively. This lesson changed my entire approach to communication.

Once, while presenting to him the diversity strategy status update and goals, he had lost interest in what I was saying. I didn't notice. Eventually, he stopped me midstream and said the following:

"I am sure that you are passionate about what you are talking about and I am all for diversity. However, right now, I am concerned with meeting my budget, maintaining our quality and safety standards and ensuring that we meet our performance goals. If you can tell me how what you are talking about is going to help me with those problems, what you say, although probably important, will not stick."

He went on to say:

"I have not seen anyone in your role help us understand that connection. If you can learn to do that, you will have everyone's attention and full engagement."

Fortunately, it was only the two of us in the room at the time. If others had been there, I think his statement would have had a very different impact on me. Instead, I was both taken aback, but a little curious about what he'd stated. In hindsight, I don't think he would have said that if others were present. He appeared to have a high level of professionalism and was held in high regard with senior leaders. My impression was that he was not the type who would have felt pleasure in pulling me out on the carpet in public.

That being said, I have to tell you, hearing this from a prominent leader in our organization was quite alarming. Many thoughts went flying through my mind (some were not so pleasant either I must confess).

I had to pause for a moment to regain my composure. Quickly playing back his words in my head, I realized that he was right and that I had made a colossal mistake. In preparing my presentation I had wanted to share with him what we were doing for diversity so badly that I had not taken the time to consider what my audience wanted to know from their own priority list of needs. He was right. My passion overcame my purpose. Thus, my audience was left out in the cold.

Realizing that this could either be a moment to create bad blood between us or it could be a real coaching/teaching moment, I decided to make it the teaching moment it was and made a mental note of it. Then I did something I had never done before. I closed the binder I had been presenting from and told him he was right. I did not come prepared to answer those problems. I asked for him to do me a favor by allowing me to reschedule our meeting. I wanted to return when I had the information he required. Surprisingly, he looked relieved and I must admit, seemed a bit proud of himself. He wholeheartedly agreed to the favor. The funny thing is that I later learned that he was actually proud of me for having admitted to this mistake.

He complimented me on my courage to admit fault. This act broke down a wall between us and he instantly became a mentor. I asked him to explain his issues and how they impacted the business from his perspective. I realized that he had complex problems that were coming at him daily. If he couldn't see how something was going to alleviate the issues he was confronted with, he didn't have the time for it.

He took the time to tell me that executives have so much on their minds, especially when managing the many problems they encounter, that it is very challenging to care about other things if you don't see how they are going to help with today's and tomorrow's problems.

He taught me that when it came to communicating strategies, etc., the goal is to make your audience care through communicating in a way that helps them meet their needs.

That lesson changed my communication skills dramatically. I went back to him two weeks later and "knocked his socks off " as he stated. I considered my audience and delivered my presentation by answering each of his issues and shared with him the many ways that diversity could contribute substantially to solutions. I have utilized this lesson-learned to this day.

Extra Toppings to Enhance Your Sandwich

◎ Focus on your nonverbal communication

◎ Consider your audience

◎ Practice is imperative

◎ Learn how to communicate by getting a coach

◎ Find ways to evaluate your performance by getting feedback and through self-evaluation

chapter twelve

Sure-fire Ingredient #9
Strategy & Execution

"When it comes to execution, it boils down to three things: knowing what to focus on and when, assigning details to the right people and influencing the right individuals and teams to get it done."
-Jocelyn

EXECUTIVE CHEF

Karen Williams | Executive Director, Strategy Implementation, Applebee's

A Straightforward Discussion on Strategy and Execution with Karen Williams, Executive Director of Strategy Implementation, Applebee's

"Most people think of strategy as this grandiose idea. However the truth is, being strategic is about being thoughtful, being analytical and keeping

things moving forward. You have to be able to look at all the different pieces to drive results, and see where the gaps are."

- Karen Williams

I met Karen through my connection with Lisbeth McNabb. (a great example of networking and relationships). Lisbeth, who is the executive chef for Supportive Networks in Chapter 8, referred Karen to me as someone who understood strategy and execution.

Lisbeth stated that, "Karen has a successful track record of implementing strategies and getting things done." She was insistent that the two of us connect, so she made the introduction.

Karen is a busy woman with family obligations and she travels a lot. However, she did not hesitate to offer her support of this book. In fact, her prompt response via email was," Glad to help."

The day Karen and I spoke, we immediately connected. Within five minutes, we discovered that we had a lot in common. To start, we both had to sneak away from our families to make our phone call. We talked about being professional women, balancing work, family and life while trying to do our share of giving back.

Our candid discussion about strategy and execution was enlightening. It was very evident *that Karen was an expert and had learned a lot on her journey.*

KAREN'S CAREER JOURNEY

Karen is a Stanford engineer with an MBA from Harvard University. Her experience spans all aspects of the value chain, working from strategic blueprinting to product development in both Fortune 500 and small to mid-cap companies. Known as a change agent, she is particularly adept at translating vision into reality.

In college, Karen pursued an engineering track based on her father's influence. Her father thought that a degree in engineering would ensure that she could get a job. However, Karen developed an interest in product design, a combination of chemical and industrial design. Karen described product design as making devices and systems with the human factor (people) in mind.

While in business school, Karen read about a research study that focused on the question, "How do you replicate success?" She found this topic of interest and was lucky enough to work with the leaders who were studying this concept.

Learning about how to drive results and what the components are that make you successful was intriguing. This was her early indicator that she had a passion for understanding what made for successful strategies and executions.

Karen's career included working for Pepsico in Supply Chain Management. There she worked in program management and production. Her job was to manage the product flow from beginning to end. However, it was at The Corner Bakery that she discovered her strength in strategy.

The Corner Bakery was a risky career move. There she accepted the position of chief financial officer without having a finance background. Not many women would have had the courage to take such a leap.

"Risk taking" is a required competency if you wish to make it to the C-suite. This role was challenging but it gave me a broad aspect of the business that was extremely beneficial in my career."   -Karen

Her current role as the executive director, Strategy and Implementation, at Applebee's allows her to blend both her creative and strategic sides to getting things done. This allows her to impact the business in significant ways and what she enjoys the most.

KAREN'S PERSPECTIVE ON STRATEGY AND EXECUTION
(in her words)

Execution is critical to career success. Without execution, you are not going to be the "go to person," the person that makes things happen or is seen as the person who can be trusted for results. Execution requires one to think strategically. When one is thinking strategically, it is like saying to yourself:

'This is where I am; this is where I want to go; now where are the gaps, what are my strengths, and what do I need to do to get there?'

Your ability to execute effectively has a lot to do with your reputation in your network and your ability to influence. Both of these components are critical and linked together. When it comes to execution, some people lack the self-awareness on how their inability to get things done impacts their relationships. If you can't get things done, people will learn to work around you.

Another important thing about execution is having a basic sense of what comes first and figuring out where you have problems. One main problem I see with people and execution is most people seem to work from front to back. In other words, they work in linear steps like the solution to the problem will be laid out perfectly one step at a time. Most of the time, finding solutions is not a clean process and the first step is not always clear.

Women suffer from this most often. We tend to wait until we have the perfect answer instead of trusting our gut and picking a place to start. It took me a long time to learn this. Believe it or not, 80% of the time, our gut is right. We just need to put our strategy down on paper and then edit it as we go along. Trying to come up with perfection before you start paralyzes people. You can implement a strategy and tweak it while in motion. Getting into motion is the important part of strategy.

Many of us believe we are strategic, but most of us just have ideas. I often ask, where is the data? Strategy is hard grunt work that is not sexy. It is about getting it done and bringing the idea to fruition.

In strategy, you need to learn how to influence what happens upstream (information, products, reputation that goes to top executives to be successful downstream (supply chain).

The book "How to Win Friends and Influence People," by Dale Carnegie, changed my career. What I learned from that book is that when you are executing or getting something done, you must consider how what you are doing will impact others. When you make it about other people, you are being strategic.

Keep in mind that you have to have the credentials, the presence and a story to back you up if you wish to be successful. If you can't execute and show qualitative results, you don't have a story.

"Innovation is nice, but it's really about execution. Innovation without execution is just an idea."
–Reid Schneider, Gaming Industry Executive Producer

WHAT IS EXECUTION?

Execution: *The performance or the act of performing; of doing something successfully; using knowledge as distinguished from merely possessing it." –Wikipedia*

This definition of execution makes it clear that "doing something successfully" is not about possessing the knowledge, but using the knowledge instead. Just because you know how to do something, doesn't mean you should be doing it. Using your knowledge strategically to get the job done through others so that you get to lead is important in executive positions.

Execution; The Discipline of Getting Things Done by Larry Bossidy and Ram Charan put it this way:

"Organizations don't execute unless the right people, individually and collectively, focus on the right details at the right time. For you as a leader, moving from the concept to the critical details is a long journey. You have to review a wide array of facts and ideas. You have to discuss what risks to take and where. You have to thread through these details, selecting those that count.

You have to assign them to the people who matter, and make sure which key ones must synchronize their work."

When I came across that statement, I admit that I read it twice before it made sense. This is how I interpreted it: When it comes to execution, leadership is about three things:

1. Knowing what details to focus on, and when
2. Knowing to whom to assign the details
3. Knowing how to influence individuals and finding the right teams to get the details done

The above sounds easy right? Wrong. Effective execution takes a lot of work and a strategic approach. It is one of the most challenging leadership competencies for women. It requires us to understand that leadership comes with more than just the responsibility of managing people. The responsibility also comes with various objectives, competing priorities, and short deadlines. Limited resources, budgets and time come with the territory as well. On top of all of that, leaders are expected to get the job done, and to execute for results. Executing with all that other stuff on your plate can be distracting.

Leadership comes with a lot of baggage too. Therefore, it is burdensome. Many leaders' scope of work is ever increasing, and resources are ever decreasing. I don't have to tell you that learning how to be successful considering these dynamics is a lot to take on.

LEADERSHIP EFFECTIVENESS IS RATED ON EXECUTION

A true leader's effectiveness is determined on how well he or she executes. Using knowledge to get the job done successfully is what sets great leaders apart from mediocre ones. There are many theories on the topic of effective leadership and execution.

One key to getting things done is delegation. Delegating effectively has propelled many women forward while leaving others in the dust. If you can master effective delegation, you will see doors open for you in ways that you could never imagine. Learning the art of delegation was one of the most significant contributors to my career advancement.

Delegation is indeed an art and one must understand the components to perform effectively. The word delegate is actually a Latin term that means, "to send from." Therefore, delegation is actually about sending work from you to someone else. When it comes to delegation, work flows through you, and onto others. Take a minute to visualize that by closing your eyes and imagining work flowing through you onto someone else. That exercise helped me really see what delegation is all about. Try it, I bet it will change how you view your job, especially if you are a leader or have aspirations to be one.

Delegation may be done in many ways and contrary to popular belief, you do not have to have direct reports to delegate. I have delegated to other departments, volunteers, students and consultants. The point is to empower others and seek their support to get the job done.

There are many positive reasons to start delegating. They are as follows:

1. Delegation will free you up to focus on more important tasks
2. Delegation will allow you to demonstrate your leadership potential
3. Delegation will help you develop others

Many women tell me that they struggle with delegation. A great example of an effective delegator was business executive J. Paul Getty. Getty was an American industrialist who in 1957 was one of the first billionaires in American history. He founded Getty Oil and built his fortune as an oil tycoon. Mr. Getty was known for sharing leadership/ entrepreneur advice. He once stated:

"It doesn't make much difference how much other knowledge or experience an executive possess; if he is unable to achieve results through people, he is worthless as an executive."

THE ART OF DELEGATION

Before we talk about how to delegate, let's talk about what delegation is and what it is not.
Delegation is...

• An assignment that comes with authority. This means that when you delegate, you also delegate the authority of the other person to make decisions.

• A vertical and horizontal process. In the past, delegation used to be solely vertical, with superiors delegating down to subordinates. Today, leaders delegate horizontally as well and to those who may not report to them.

Delegation is not…

• Just assigning tasks. Delegation involves assigning responsibility, and something that you, as the leader would normally do.

• Getting those undesirable tasks off your desk. Nothing will disengage an employee more than when they feel they are being dumped upon.

• Giving away accountability. Although you delegate responsibility, ultimate accountability continues to belong to the leader. You are responsible for the outcomes at the end of the day.

TEN STEPS TO EFFECTIVE DELEGATION

1. Determine what to delegate
2. Choose the right person, with the right skills and experience
3. Give an overview of the assignment including its importance
4. Describe the responsibility in detail

5. Solicit questions, reactions, and suggestions
6. Welcome employee's comments
7. Ask for the employee's commitment and offer to provide help, if needed
8. Be encouraging and motivating
9. Establish checkpoints with employee
10. Recognize and reward successful completion and provide feedback

KNOWING WHEN NOT TO DELEGATE IS IMPORTANT

Although delegation is important in effective execution, knowing when not to delegate is just as important. Whitney Johnson, an institutional investor all-star, guest blogger for *Harvard Business Review* and co-founder of Rosa Parks Advisors, attributes her leadership success to her understanding of proper delegation.

According to Ms. Johnson, in her 2010, article, *"3 Reasons Not to Delegate,"* before delegating, it is important to ask oneself the following three questions:

1. *Are you struggling to explain precisely what you want the delegate to do?*

2. *Are you putting your own development or ability to lead in jeopardy by delegating?*

3. *Are you potentially undermining a project's success by delegating?*

If you answer yes to any one of these questions, then you should not delegate. The task should belong solely to you for execution.

When delegating, it is crucial that you fully understand all of the details of the project and can articulate them to your delegate. It is also important to know if by delegating you stand to miss out on opportunities to learn new skills or build critical relationships. Lastly, certain high stakes projects may require you to carry them out. You must be able to ascertain when you are the best person for the job.

In closing, strategy and execution is critical to career success, especially when you make it to the executive ranks. It is this ability that allows people to break through and sustain effective careers. Execution is not easy and takes the understanding and proficiency in delegation, strategy, and influential leadership. All of these components don't usually come easy. However, when you master this sure-fire ingredient, you will be sought after and have a sustainable successful career.

Extra Toppings
to Enhance
Your Sandwich

◎ Use your knowledge to get the job done
◎ Break down projects by who, what, when and how
◎ Use influence and delegation to get others to get
   the job done
◎ Understand that execution is sometimes trusting
   your gut and reassessing along the way
◎ Know that sometimes the perfect answer doesn't
   exist. Make a decision and make it work

Sure-fire Ingredient #10
Influence Over Others

"The true measure of leadership comes when it's acquired through "influence" and followers follow, not because they have to, but because they want to.
-Jocelyn

EXECUTIVE CHEF

Nancy M. Schlichting | CEO, Henry Ford Health System

An Enlightening Discussion on Influential Leadership with Nancy M. Schlichting, CEO, Henry Ford Health System

"Influence becomes increasingly more important over your career. I recall early on, employees would come to me to help them with things; even when I was in lower level positions. When people seek you out, that is when you know you have influence. You don't need a title to be influential."
-Nancy Schlichting

Having had the privilege to work under Nancy Schlichting's leadership is something that I never took for granted. My first encounter with Nancy was at a senior leadership meeting we had scheduled to talk about our Affirmative Action plan and diversity recruitment strategy. At the time, she was the president and CEO of Henry Ford Hospital in Detroit, Michigan , the flagship of the Henry Ford Health System. It was 2003 and my second week on the job.

The meeting was held in the executive boardroom at the hospital. As I was searching for the right seat to park myself, Nancy walked in the room. Immediately by her presence, I knew I was among an exceptional leader. Her confidence, grace and a sense of calmness left me captivated. She led the meeting with tremendous influence and power, and everyone was engaged. She treated each one at the table with respect regardless of level.

Nancy also impressed me when although she was extremely busy, she had obviously read the material I supplied prior to the meeting and came prepared to ask questions. This practice sent a message that not only was she an exceptional leader, but that she was committed to the topic. This made me feel valued as well for it was my work that she had given time and attention.

With open arms she welcomed me as a new member to the organization. Her smile was sincere and her demeanor communicated competence, integrity and openness. I was confident that she was a leader from whom I could learn a great deal. From that moment on, although she never knew it, she became my "silent mentor."

NANCY'S CAREER JOURNEY

Nancy became a chief operating officer, COO at the young age of 28. Running a 650-bed hospital in Akron, Ohio, it was a role that came with broad-based responsibilities including all operational areas, Human Resources and Finance. According to Nancy, it was her colleagues who persuaded her to put her name in the hat after the previous COO left the hospital.

With their coaxing, Nancy wrote a letter to her potential boss about her vision and how she could change the direction of the hospital. After receiving the letter, her potential boss sent her to interview with a search consultant who put her through a tough interview. Surprisingly, the consultant thought the 28 year-old Nancy could do the job and referred her as a candidate. With the endorsement of the board, she got the job.

Nancy joined Henry Ford Health System in 1998 as senior vice president and chief administrative officer. She was promoted to executive vice president and chief operating officer the following year and assumed the additional responsibility of president and CEO of Henry Ford Hospital in 2001.

Prior to joining Henry Ford Health System, Schlichting was executive vice president and chief operating officer of Summa Health System in Akron, Ohio. She has also served as president of the Eastern Region of Catholic Health Initiatives, president and chief executive officer of Riverside Methodist Hospitals, and executive vice president and chief operating officer of Akron City Hospital.

Schlichting earned her bachelor's in public policy studies from Duke University where she graduated magna cum laude. She received her Masters in Business Administration in Hospital Administration and Accounting from Cornell University. She served her Administrative Residency at Memorial Sloan-Kettering Cancer Center and her Administrative Fellowship at the American Hospital Association/Blue Cross Blue Shield Association. She has also completed a Healthier Communities Fellowship with the Health Care Forum.

Recently Schlichting was selected as one of the nation's top 25 female health care executives by *Modern Healthcare*, a sister publication of *Crain's Detroit Business*. It was the second time that the magazine had recognized her. *Modern Healthcare* cited some of Schlichting's achievements as:

• Revamping Henry Ford's urology program and
 approving the purchase of a $1 million da Vinci robot system to perform minimally invasive prostate cancer surgery.

• Opening a $360 million hospital in West Bloomfield Township.

• Completing a $310 million overhaul of *Henry Ford Hospital* in Detroit.

NANCY'S PERSPECTIVE ON INFLUENCE AND LEADERSHIP *(in her words)*

You can influence based on the respect that people have for you. That respect is earned every day. It is not something that you win. It is earned by the high level of competence in what you do. People believe what you say because you have the credibility that guides what you think. You are thoughtful, you reason well, you think clearly. Your character plays an important role as well. It is how you relate to people and how you respect them. You get respect because you respect others. For sustained influence, you have to be able to demonstrate and relate in ways that show your competence and character.

Influence is also gained by your track record of performance. A track record of making good decisions and having good judgment will help influence others to follow your lead. When your track record is good, then when you say something, people will listen. When they listen, then you can influence what they think and how they are going to behave.

I have never thought of myself as having power. I think of myself as having an enormous privilege to lead. This privilege gives me the opportunity to create strategies for an organization and leave it in a different way than it was before I was there.

The higher you go, the more risky it becomes. For one thing, you can get fired, or worse, you can ruin an organization. When I get up in the morning, I feel responsible for thousands of employees and millions of patients. I also feel responsible for the financial risks. Therefore, high-level leadership is not for the faint of heart.

Often leaders treat employees like children whenever they have to deliver bad news. Answering the "why" you made this decision helps people understand and the support you get from this approach is amazing.

I love working with staff at all levels of employment in the organization. The reason I am in this work is because I care deeply about the patient's, physician's and employee's experience. If I didn't care, I would get drained. Interacting with our employees invigorates me. To ensure that I connect with as many employees as possible, I make a list every summer. In August I go visiting places so that I can interact with employees where I don't normally get to be. It is great to get to let people know who I am. I never wanted to be a faceless corporate type, like the name you see on a check, but you don't know who they are.

Some leaders are born with influence. Others learn to lead later in life. There is no one answer to that. Often we learn from what we see. I learn more from bad leaders and it taught me what I didn't want to do.

There are a lot of people who can influence. Therefore, not all influencers are leaders. Informal leaders can influence too. Leaders and influencers are not one in the same. In fact, one of the most important things when it comes to influence on kids is whom they hang around with. If they hang with kids who do their homework, or are physically active or eat healthy, they tend to be the same way.

My mom paid a lot of attention to who our friends were and would not allow us to go to anyone's house until she met them first. She even had our teachers over our house so that she could get to know them first too as she knew of their influence on us as well.

Many of the ways I interact with people I learned from my mother. When we went to the grocery store, for instance, it took forever to get out of the store. My mother would talk to the butcher, the produce person, the cashier, the manager, etc. Of course they treated her well because she was interested in them. This was a great lesson for me as a kid. I learned that when you treat people with dignity and respect, no matter what their job is, it is a wonderful way to connect.

My mother, by far was the most influential person in my life without a doubt. She shaped my leadership instinct, my people instincts and my work ethic. She was a slave driver when it came to schoolwork.

Influence comes from how I treat people. People know that I care about them. When you care for others, you don't want to let them down. I love the people I work with. You spend so many hours at work and we go through a lot. When you get to know people and they know you care about them as a person, they will go through a fire for you. When people know that you care, it also makes for a great working environment. Treating people as individuals and putting each person first are important.

I am fortunate to posses the talent of remembering names. If I have meaningful conversation with a person, it is easier to remember their names. Know your people, what makes them tick. If you know each person well, they will do a great job for you.

Early in your career it is important not to be passive. Be creative, put forth your ideas, dig deep, and bring something new to the conversation. That is when people listen. If you think about things differently and put your ideas out there, that is when you can become influential.

NANCY'S OTHER LESSONS LEARNED AND ADVICE

Basic human relationships are the core of everything in life. So many leaders don't get that. Many leaders focus on the finance. That is why we focus on people first and know the rest will come. If I can't create the right environment, I don't know what I am here for. It is all about people.

The fun thing about a career is that you don't always know what's around the corner. Seize opportunity or make opportunity. When I think of my career, I couldn't have predicted the outcome. You get to a certain age and you don't have to look back. You look forward.

At the end of the day, we are all responsible for our own careers. Organizations however, are responsible for providing resources.

When it comes to women in executive leadership roles, I can name on one hand, the number of women running health systems. I feel the importance to demonstrate an example of leadership that is encouraging to women to enter the field, especially for young people.

WHAT IS INFLUENTIAL LEADERSHIP?

Initially I was prepared to call this chapter, simply "leadership" until I came across a term that caused me to pause. The term was *influential leadership*. The first time I heard of the term, the thought that came to mind was, *"What's the difference between leaders and influential leaders?" Is there really a big difference that would warrant adding this ingredient to the cookbook?* In my search to find the answer, I came across an interesting definition from a doctoral student whom I only know as *"Ann."* I came across Ann on a blog site hosted by Steve Pavlina at www.stevepavlina.com. Ann was researching the definition of influential leadership for her thesis and below is the definition she came up with:

"Influential leadership is the type of leadership that creates followers who want to follow as opposed to followers who believe that they have to follow."

After reading Ann's definition, it was apparent to me that there is indeed a big difference between leaders who lead through leadership and leaders who lead through influence. Just because you have a title of leader, doesn't mean that people want and will follow you.

It is through actual "influence" that makes people want to follow a leader. Influential leaders don't lead through rank, power or fear, the three attributes that may cause followers to believe they have to follow. Instead, like our executive chef, Nancy Schlichting, they acquire a quality that inspires, motivates and compels followers to take their lead. Therefore, influential leadership is the highest level of leaders.

So what do influential leaders have that others leaders don't? According to Ann, the doctorial student, the qualities that makes one an influential leader are as follows:

- *Charisma* - *a personal attractiveness that enables you to influence others; an ability to arouse fervent popular devotion and enthusiasm*
- *Communication* - *Communicators take something complicated and make the message simple*
- *Integrity* - *being consistently honest, forthright, and ethical; doing what they say and saying what they do. They walk their talk. Followers need to be able to trust the leader, and without that trust, influence is impossible*
- *Passion* - *Every leader who is passionate about what he/she does is on a mission to share it with the world*
- *Authenticity* - *Leaders genuinely desire to serve others through their leadership. They are more*

interested in empowering the people they lead to make a difference than they are in power, money, or prestige for themselves. They are as guided by qualities of the heart, by passion and compassion, as they are by qualities of the mind

- **Servant hood** - *Leaders want to be of value to others, contributing to the benefts of others, whether it is their employees, their business, their industry, their family, or their peers*

When it comes to influential leadership, there is no magic pill, no quick fix, and no glory without pain. It takes work, commitment and perseverance. Contrary to what many may believe, or shall I say hope, influential leadership does not happen overnight. Most successful leaders, who gain this level of leadership, have worked decades or more developing their skills. Through continuous learning, improvement and dedication, they reach a level that only a few have truly mastered. Therefore, if you wish to reach this level of leadership, it will require a focused effort on your part.

There are many things that stand in the way of understanding the true meaning of leadership. One major reason is many professionals don't understand the difference between leading and managing. Many of us still have a difficult time distinguishing between the two and more times than not, we believe that we are leading when we are actually only managing. I see this happen with many women.

While searching Wikipedia, (my best friend), I found definitions of both management and leadership as follows:

"Management in all business and organizational activities is the act of getting people together to accomplish desired goals and objectives using available resources efficiently and effectively.

Management comprises planning, organizing, staffing, leading or directing, and controlling an organization or effort for the purpose of accomplishing a goal."

Leadership on the other hand is described as:

"Leadership is the process of <u>social influence</u> in which one person can enlist the aid and support of others in the accomplishment of a common task."

Taking these two definitions into consideration, an apparent difference emerges. Basically, managing is about organizing people and processes to move in a desired direction. Leadership on the other hand, is about creating the way or "change" to influence others to willingly contribute to your cause.

INFLUENTIAL LEADERSHIP IS ABOUT GETTING OTHERS TO WANT TO FOLLOW YOU WHEN THEY DON'T HAVE TO

The leadership proverb, *"He who thinks he leads, but has no followers, is only taking a walk,"* helps me put into perspective what leadership is. Getting people to follow, especially when they don't have to due to fear, power etc, is true influence. In the book, *Influencer; The Power to Change Anything,* by Patterson, Grenny and Maxfield, states,

> **"Once you tap into the power of influence, you can reach out and help others work smarter and grow faster. The sky is the limit for an influencer."**

Imagine if everyone who worked for you were able to work smarter and faster. Would you then be able to execute? Probably, yes.

John Maxwell, America's expert on leadership, and author of several leadership books, has developed what he calls the *5 Levels of Leadership.* In his book, *Leadership 101, What Every Leader Needs to Know,* Maxwell states that in order to acquire influence, a leader must advance through several leadership levels. The levels are as follows:

1. *Position*
2. *Permission*
3. *Production*
4. *People Development*
5. *Personhood*

In these five levels of leadership, Maxwell believes influence may be gained by understanding how the levels work within leadership. According to Maxwell:

Level 1: Position, people follow you because they have to due to your position. However, your influence will not go beyond your position power if you stay at this level.

Level 2: Permission, people start to follow you because they want to. It is at this level that relationships are built. People enjoy working under your leadership. They feel appreciated and valued. Empathy, recognition and individualism are important at this level.

Level 3: Production, people want to follow because they can see results and what your leadership has done for the organization. This is the level where what you produce, (good quality outcomes) is what keeps people engaged. Accountability for results for both the team and leader is important.

Level 4: People Development, in this level, people follow because of what they get personally from your leadership. It is only when people feel that they are gaining from following that one reaching this level. Personal growth and development is what keeps followers engaged. According to Maxwell, this is a critical level.

Lastly, **Level 5: Personhood**, this is the ultimate level that few reach. After many successful years of growing and developing others that you earn respect. Leaders whom reach this level of influence are followed due to the person they have become.

There are other theories on how one becomes influential. Alan Keith, a former corporate finance director at biotech firm Genentech, and leadership guru in his report, *"The Five Practices of Exemplary Leadership"* *states that,*

> ***"Leadership is ultimately about creating a way for people to contribute to making something extraordinary happen."***

According to Mr. Keith, when getting extraordinary things done in organizations, leaders engage in these *"Five Practices and Ten Commandments of Leadership":*

Model the Way
1. Clarify values by finding your voice and affirming shared ideals.
2. Set the example by aligning actions with shared values.

Inspire a Shared Vision

3. Envision the future by imagining exciting and ennobling possibilities.
4. Enlist others in a common vision by appealing to shared aspirations.

Challenge the Process

5. Search for opportunities by seizing the initiative and by looking outward for innovative ways to improve.
6. Experiment and take risks by constantly generating small wins and learning from experience.

Enable Others to Act

7. Foster collaboration by building trust and facilitating relationships.
8. Strengthen others by increasing self-determination and developing competence.

Encourage the Heart

9. Recognize contributions by showing appreciation for individual excellence.
10. Celebrate the values and victories by creating a spirit of community.

Taking Mr. Keith's theory on exemplary leadership into consideration, what sets influential leaders apart from others is their willingness to role model their beliefs. Therefore, these types of leaders don't just rattle off a list of values. They demonstrate those values in their daily interactions.

Influential leaders are also adept at painting clear pictures about their vision for the future that excites and inspires others to embrace and/or own the vision. They describe their vision using descriptive words and positive emotions that compel others to want to be a part of it. By looking outside themselves and organizations, influential leaders create environments that promote innovation by breaking down walls to collaboration, encouraging experimentation, and encouraging risk taking. This also sounds a lot like what our executive chef, Nancy Schlichting described.

Another distinction in influential leadership is the fostering of personal accountability and trust. Leaders, who possess influence, convey their confidence in others to get the job done and give the autonomy to make decisions to the owners. They feed the souls of their followers through their genuine care for others and recognition of jobs well done. According to our executive chef in the chapter on *Effective Relationships*, Gerard Van Grinsven has strong feeling about influential leadership.

During our interview he stated the following:

"When you are a leader of influence, you don't run around being a micromanager, controlling everything and telling everyone what to do. Instead you let go and hand over control. Leaders become a man or woman of influence and bring out the best in their people. They encourage them and let them soar.

How do you become a man or woman of influence? You do it through relationships. When you have strong relationships, others will seek your council, advice and want to be a part of your life. When you are seen as a control freak, people will not come to you.

Be a leader of influence beyond the walls of the organization. Ask yourself: Can you become a parent of influence or a parent who manages? How can you make your children or community feel that they can soar and make a bigger impact?

You can tell a leader of influence by the way they hold themselves, their posture and how they talk. If they cannot look me in the eye, or they look stressed or they are cautious about what they say to me because I am the CEO, then I know I have a manager in front of me. On the contrary, when they walk with eyes full of fire, they look you in the eye and they can't wait to tell you how they can't wait to make a difference, then I know I have a leader with influence in front of me."

A HOT PASTRAMI SANDWICH STORY

Tricia, a woman I met at one of my workshops, approached me during the break, to complain about how she had been overlooked for a promotion; a promotion she felt entitled to because of her many years of commitment to and sacrifice on behalf of the company. She was extremely miffed that she had labored countless hours to redesign the company's entire talent selection process.

According to Tricia, she had singlehandedly implemented a new procedure that revolutionized how the company recruited new talent. Her many innovations, and hard work contributed successfully to the company's bottom line. Due to the importance of the recruitment project, she had worked countless hours benchmarking, testing, and motivating her team. She was almost in tears as she spoke about how she had 'devoted her entire life to that project.' As I listened to her story, I was struck by her deep-rooted pain, bitterness and overwhelming sense of betrayal. With venom in her voice, she told me how she wasn't even considered for the promotion. And, because her work was " flawless" and she made sure that every detail was precise, leaving no stone unturned, she could not understand why a fairly new manager brought in just two years prior, was promoted over her. On top of that, the new manager had less than half of the experience that she had and his job responsibilities were far less demanding than hers. Tricia described him as a "brownnoser; always kissing up to the senior executives. Always bragging about what he was doing."

Ready to quit, she was desperate to know what caused her to be overlooked. She was desperate for answers and needed to know what she had done wrong. Since she believed that her team's success was all attributed to her strong leadership, she couldn't understand why her superiors didn't see her as a strong candidate.

Tricia's problem was revealed at the very start of her story. When she said that she "singlehandedly" implemented the new procedure for the company's recruiting project, a red flag was revealed. Most of her work was done in isolation and without influence. What Tricia didn't realize was that by not including others in the recruiting project, she sent a message to upper management that her current position was the right one for her, not the promotional opportunity. She proved that she is the right person to continue to produce projects that require singlehanded attention and devotion to detail. Tricia is in fact a doer, not an influencer. Although she was able to get the job done, she didn't demonstrate her ability to use influence to get it done. A leader without influence is one who manages a project, not leads it.

If her leaders were savvy, I am sure they came to a similar conclusion. On the other hand her competitor demonstrated that level of influential leadership. Instead, Tricia saw his influence as being a brown-noser.

When it comes to leadership, organizations expect their leaders to execute and get the job done. However, the key to success in leadership is about learning how to get the job done through influence. Many women believe that they alone must possess the technical skills and "know how" to get the job done and unfortunately they continue to hold this misguided belief throughout their careers. Women of color are even more apt to be firm believers in this concept. Early in careers, technical abilities are indeed important. However, as your career advances, technical skills are less significant, while influence and relationships are.

HOW BEING A MANAGER GETS IN THE WAY OF OUR RISE TO HIGHER LEADERSHIP RANKS

In the January 2011, *Harvard Business Review* article, "*Stop Holding Yourself Back; Five ways People Unwittingly*

Sabotage Their Rise to Leadership," an interesting perspective on how self-preservation impacts career advancement is discussed. According to the article,

"True leadership is about making other people better as a result of your presence and making sure your impact endures in your absence."

Most women are concerned with self-preservation. Therefore, when many of us obtain a leadership position, we set out to prove that our team is good because of us. Our focus is on demonstrating our skill set for managing the team.   Being involved in all aspects of the projects assigned to us, knowing details, and rolling our sleeves up is our common approach. Most women leaders I've observed can tell you every little detail about the work being performed under their leadership.

Often in my leadership roles, I used to be the same way. There was a need for me to show that "I knew my stuff." This caused me to get deeply involved in projects, which required a lot of energy, time and commitment. This level of focus took me away from opportunities to build relationships with colleagues, stakeholders and my community networks, all of which is necessary to advance in leadership. Instead, we keep our nose to the grindstone and our hands in the details.

The need for self-preservation also prevents us from showing our vulnerabilities and for asking for help. We feel compelled to show that we are competent and can find our own solutions. Therefore, we seldom reach out for support. Instead we focus on building our technical skills, so that we are proficient in our disciplines. Keeping current skills is important. However, as you move up the ladder, technical skills become less important. It's your influential skills and focus on making others better that help move you to higher ranks.

Self-preservation also leads to playing it safe. In other words, the fear of making bad decisions prevents us from taking risks. We seldom challenge the status quo and wait for permission and/or order to take action.

SO, WHAT DOES IT TAKE TO BE AN INFLUENTIAL LEADER?

Influencing others is not just about getting people to do something. It is about getting them to "want" to do it and feel good in the process. How do you do that? In the research article by 2011 *Harvard Business Review* (HBR), titled, *"Are you a Good Boss-or A Great One?"* there are three imperatives to becoming a influential leader. They are,

1. *Managing yourself*
2. *Managing your network*
3. *Managing your team*

According to HBR, when it comes to *"managing oneself,"* it's all about building trust in your followers that you can do the job; that you have strong values and that you are committed. People watch your every move ensuring that your actions match your words.

In terms of *"managing your network,"* it is about understanding and "operating effectively" in organizational politics. Building relationships with influential supporters and potential enemies is critical to obtaining influence. Having a diverse supportive network will strengthen your influence by building extra support around you.

When it comes to *"managing your team,"* is all about making expectations clear to each team member and how they contribute individually and as part of the team. Each member must understand his or her role in contributing to the common cause.

The article goes on to state the importance of self-evaluation to keep a pulse on how well you are performing. As you rise up in organizations, you will receive less feedback. Therefore, you must learn to conduct your own self-assessments.

At the end of the day, influential leadership is about making the world a better place and inspiring others to move forward. It is also about building trust and growing others to be the best that they can be. Influential leaders live their values, and go day-to-day with integrity, commitment and accountability. They use their power effectively and make others feel fortunate to be under their influential leadership.

What I've Learned...

"Career success isn't something that's handed out at graduation with your diploma. Success is something that you earn through working smart, being courageous and having determination. No one starts at the top, so be prepared to pay your dues." - Jocelyn

IN CLOSING,

Remember that a successful career always starts with a strategy and a plan for advancement. However, even with a strategy, most only become successful, when preparation, opportunity and luck come together. So be sure to prepare, and start building your career strategy sandwich today. Who knows, maybe you will be lucky enough, to be in the right place, and at the right time, to take advantage of some great opportunities.

I like to thank you again for joining me. And please, know that if you have any questions, comments or feedback; feel free to email me at

jgiangrande@sashewomen.com

It would be my pleasure to assist you, in any way I can.

Until next time, good luck with your career. I look forward to connecting again. Get cooking!

Take care.

Brought to you by SASHE, LLC.

Helping professional women build the confidence to unlock their potential.

For information on how to bring Jocelyn to your organization, bulk book discounts and free resources, visit www.JocelynGiangrande.com

NOTE FROM THE AUTHOR

I am Jocelyn Giangrande (means big John in Italian), and I live with my husband Nick, and teenage son, Quen, in the beautiful state of Michigan.

My proudest accomplishment is my family. We are happy, healthy and close. My husband and I recently celebrated our 16th wedding anniversary and we've been together for the last 18 years. If there is such a thing as a soul mate, he is mine. As for my son, I couldn't ask for anyone better. He is a smart young man who enjoys correcting me every chance he gets. I'm amazed by his intellect and convinced his smarts come from my side of the family.

Born in Boston, I am the middle child of three and was raised by a loving, hardworking mother who created a rich life for all of us. My mother worked diligently to surround us with love, education and great experiences. She was a wiz at shielding the fact that we didn't have much money. Many people would have considered us to be poor. However, I always felt rich in our home.

I love learning new things and enjoyed college. My undergraduate degree came from Colby College, in Waterville, Maine where I earned a B. A. degree in psychology. I also attended Marygrove College in Detroit, Michigan where I earned a M.A. in Human Resources Administration. The last 15 years of my career have been in corporate America.

At the end of the day, my most rewarding passion is helping others to be the best they can be. The joy I get from seeing the best in everyone I meet, is something I can't quite explain. I just love working with others, helping to bring out their talents, strengths and qualities. Building confidence and unlocking potential is my specialty. I know this is my calling and I will do my part to share it with those whom find it useful.

If I may support you on your journey, reach out and contact me. It would be my pleasure to work with you. Together, let's move forward.

Take care,

Jocelyn

jgiangrande@sashewomen.com

Jocelyn's Quotes of Motivation, Encouragement and Things to Ponder

"What I learned most during my career is that managing your career is your responsibility and yours alone."

"Advancing your career is a competitive sport. To increase your wins, you must get your mindset ready to compete."

"Most successful women's sandwiches also have 3 super ingredients in common; a lot of preparation, many opportunities and a bit of luck."

"What I learned from working in restaurants is that preparation is everything."

"No matter how much you prepare, it's getting access to opportunities that makes the difference."

" Some people just seem to have a monopoly on good luck! Being in the right place and time pays off big time!"

"You don't need to see yourself as 'better' than others. You just need to see yourself as 'just as good.'"

"Any good sandwich starts with good bread. When it comes to your career, confidence is your bread."

"Success in early careers can lead to a false sense of confidence. Many of us are promoted prematurely, without strong foundations of confidence. When we hit bumps, our careers get shaky and derail at times."

"Once your talents are focused and developed, they can be the strengths that propel you forward."

"When it comes to getting a job, rarely are you selected solely on how smart you are. You are most likely selected based on the feeling or expectation people have about you. This expectation is based on your reputation."

"I have always felt that there is nothing worse, than being successful and no one knows it."

"When it comes to networking, many of us still see it as selling ourselves to someone else, pretending to be interested in others, or asking for help when you need a job. Networking is none of that. Networking is about making connections with others, so that through your connection, you both benefit."

"Going the course is a challenging ride. Mentors with different perspectives, can help push you to grow and save you from disaster."

"The ability to build strong and affirming relationships is perhaps the most critical to overall career success."

In as brief as six seconds, others get an impression of you based on what you communicate. We must master the art of communicating confidently to remain competitive."

"The true measure of leadership comes when it's acquired through "influence", and followers follow, not because they have to, but because they want to."

"When it comes to execution, it boils down to three things: knowing what to focus on and when, assigning details to the right people and influencing the right individuals and teams to get it done."

"Career Success isn't something that's handed out at graduation with your diploma. Success is something that you earn through working smart, being courageous and having determination. No one starts at the top, so be prepared to pay your dues."

SUGGESTED RESOURCES AND INFORMATION

1. Jocelyngiangrande.com
2. Mindtool.com
3. W2Wlink.com
4. Harvard Business Review
5. Dale Carnegie Leadership Training
6. Selfgrowth.com
7. National Seminars Training (800 258-7246)
8. Toast Masters International
9. Strengthfinder.com
10. Talentplus.com
11. Henryford.com

BIBLIOGRAPHY AND RESOURCES

1. Amabile, T. M. (1983). Brilliant but cruel: Perceptions of negative evaluators. *Journal of Experimental Social Psychology, 19*(2), 146.

2. *Ferrazi, K., & Tahl, R. (2005). Never eat alone: and other secrets to success, one relationship at a time.* New York : Currency Doubleday.

3. Ibarra, H. (2010). Why men still get more promotions than women. *Harvard Business Review,* (9), 80-85.

4. Martin, C.G. (2011, February). What was your biggest break? *Oprah Magazine.*

5. Tan, C. (2009) Tall people earn more; Height, leadership and persuasion abilities. Retrieved August 22, 2009 from www. psychology@suite 101.com

6. Judge, T. A., & Cable, D. M. (2004). The effect of physical height on workplace success and income: Preliminary test of a theoretical model. *Journal of Applied Psychology, 89*(3), 428-441.

7. Greene, J. (2011, April 21). *Nancy Schlichting named one of top 25 women in health care by Modern Healthcare.* Retrieved May 2, 2011, from http://www.crainsdetroit. com/article/20110421/FREE/110429982/nancy-schlichting-named-one-of-top-25-women-in-health-care-by-modern-healthcare#

8. Mead, C. [April 21, 2011]. Profile: Nancy Schlichting, Henry Ford Health System. *Detroiter Magazine.*

9. Henry Ford Health System (2011). Nancy M. Schlichting Profile retrieved from www.henryford.com

10. Pavlina, S. (2006). Is Steve an influential leader? Retrieved from www.stevepavlina.com.

11. Keith, A. (2011, April 4). The Five Practices of Exemplary Leadership. *Genetech, 5 [pg. 1-15]*

12. Morris, A., Ely, R. J., & Frei, F.X. (2011). Managing yourself: Stop holding yourself back; Five ways people unwittingly sabotage their rise to leadership. *Harvard Business Review.[volume 1/2 Jan-Feb. 2011 Pg. 160-164]*

13. Hill, L. A., & Lineback, K. (2011). Are you a good boss or a great one? *Harvard Business Review. [volume 1/2 Jan-Feb. 2011 Pg. 124-132]*

14. Fraser, G. (2008). *Click: Ten truths for building extraordinary relationships.* New York: McGraw-Hill.

15. Giscombe, K., (2011). Building trust, between managers and diverse women direct reports. *Catalyst.* [This was a report pg. 1-10]

16. Kabani, S. (2010). *The zen of social media marketing: An easier way to build credibility, generate buss and increase revenue.* Dallas: BenBella Books.

17. www.mindtools.com

18. www.W2Wlink.com

19. Epstein, B. (2009). How to: Use Facebook for professional networking. *The Social Media Guide.* Retrieved August 14, 2009, from www.mashable.com

20. www.linkedin.com

21. www.twitter.com

22. www.facebook.com

23. Heim, P., & Golant, S. (1993). *Hardball for women, winning at the game of business.* New York: Penguin Group.

24. Patterson, K, Grenny, J., Maxfield, D., & McMillan, R. (2008). *Influencer: the power to change anything.* New York: McGraw-Hill.

25. Maxwell, J. (2002). *Leadership 101: What every leader needs to know.* Nashville: Nelson.

26. Maxwell, J. (2007). *Talent is never enough: Discover the choices that will take you beyond your talent.* New York: Nelson.

27. Bossidy, L., Charan, R., & Burck, C. (2002). *Execution: The discipline of getting things done.* New York: Crown Business.

28. Johnson, Whitney, HBR Blog Network, *3 Reasons You Shouldn't Delegate,* Dec. 2010

29. www.womenemployed.com

30. Beeson, J. (2009) Managing yourself; Why you didn't get that promotion. *Harvard Business Review.* [Volume 6 pg. 1-8]

31. Thomas, A., & Gabarro, J. (1999) *Breaking through: The making of minority executives in corporate America.* Boston: Harvard Business School Press.

32. Manktelow, J. (2003). *Mind tools: The Essential skills for an excellent career.* West Sussex: Mind Tools LTD.

33. Kanter, R. *(2004, 2006).Confidence: How winning streaks and losing streaks begin and end.* New York: Crown Publishing.

34. Gladwell, M. *(2000, 2002).The tipping point: How little things can make big things happen.* Boston: Little, Brown and Company.

35. Riley, M. Riley's Guide: The art of building alliance. *Retrieved from http://www.rileyguide.com*

36. Cohen, D., & Prusak, L. (2001). *In good company: How social capital makes organizations work.* Cambridge: Harvard Business School Press.

37. Carnegie, D.(1936) How to win friends and influence people. New York: Simon and Schuster.

38. D'Alessandro, D.(2004). Career warfare: 10 rules for building your successful brand on the business battlefield. New York: McGraw-Hill.

39. D'Alessandro, D.(2008). Executive warfare: 10 rules of engagement for winning your war for success. New York: McGraw-Hill.

40. Rath, T. *(2007.)StrengthsFinder 2.0: Now, discover your strengths.* New York: Gallup Press.

41. Griffin, J. (1998, 2008). *How to say it at work: Power words, phrases, and communication secrets for getting ahead.* New York: Prentice Hall Press, Penguin Group.

42. Mindell, P. (2001). *How to say it for women: Communicating with confidence and power using the language of success.* New York: Prentice Hall.

43. Klaus, P. (2003). *Brag! The art of tooting your own horn without blowing it.* New York: Warner Books.